Verbal Pattern in

Four Quartets:

A Close Reading

of T. S. Eliot's Poem

by

SISTER MARY ANTHONY WEINIG

Rosemont College

International Book Publishers
5213 Greendale Drive
Troy, Michigan 48098

Excerpts from *Four Quartets* by T. S. Eliot are
reprinted by permission of Harcourt Brace
Jovanovich, Inc.; copyright 1943 by T. S. Eliot;
renewed 1971 by Esme Valerie Eliot.

Copyright © 1982 by International Book Publishers, Inc.
5213 Greendale Drive
Troy, Michigan 48098

PRINTED IN THE UNITED STATES OF AMERICA

Library of Congress Card No.: 82-08233
ISBN: 0-936968-04-4

To the Society of the Holy Child Jesus

Table of Contents

Acknowledgements

Thanks are due to *Criticism* and *Greyfriars* for permission to use the portions of chapters one and four published as articles in their pages; to Harcourt Brace Jovanovich, Inc., for permission to quote *Four Quartets*; to Fordham University for permission and encouragement to publish the body of this dissertation, whose original title was "Diction, Syntax and Rhetoric in T. S. Eliot's *Four Quartets*," and whose appendix is available from University Microfilms as *A Concordance to T. S. Eliot's Four Quartets*; to Dr. Charles Donahue of happy memory, who directed the dissertation; to the Society of the Holy Child Jesus and to Rosemont College for financial assistance in bringing this work to light, as well as for more valuable and less tangible support

INTRODUCTION

The following tentative study of certain less discussed structural elements in T. S. Eliot's *Four Quartets* proposes by its examination of the technique to arrive at a better understanding of the effect of the poem, and ultimately of the poem itself. The analogy that suggests itself, that of the relation of structure to function in the biological order, carries with it a warning of the method's limitations: as anatomy and physiology fall short of conveying a complete picture of the organism to whose nature, however, they contribute many valuable clues, so the dissecting table approach to a literary work is, though in some respects necessary, of restricted value. What is offered here, positing as it does the essential rightness of Eliot, is, then, in no sense literary criticism, but a careful preparation of the cadaver for the application of the tools of comparison and analysis by more competent hands. If the tone is more aseptic than appreciative this will not seem inappropriate in view of the project's purpose, and may be welcomed as a wholesome antidote to the surfeit of interpretive comment in Eliot criticism.

The division of the subject into "diction, syntax and rhetoric" is not intended to imply that these are mutually exclusive categories. They are taken rather as successive expansions of an initial consideration of the word as vital entity participating as it were in the creative life process and sensitive to environmental modifications.

It is hoped that this introduction will establish both the validity of this viewpoint and the exact sense in which the chosen terms are to be understood. No pejorative connotation, for example, is to be attached to "rhetoric." Succeeding chapters will deal in turn with each of the *Quartets* and, on the assumption "that poetry is made with words,"[1] explore the kaleidoscopic divagations of these units with which Eliot has so often voiced his own deep pre-occupation.

The principal source of this study is of course the text of *Four Quartets*,[2] with support for many of its conclusions in *obiter dicta* gleaned from Eliot's unreprinted prose—reviews, editorials, correspondence, occasional articles—as well as from those essays he has committed to the permanence of book form. The bulk of the secondary material searched has yielded mostly negative results, a circumstance in itself favoring the pursuit of the present task. Of the major commentaries consulted during the (remote) preparation for this paper and included in the bibliography, acknowledgement is more often general than specific. Much has been absorbed in reading that may unwittingly be offered here as original. Many identifications are widely enough accepted to be considered general property and are therefore not annotated as to source.

The approach is thus relatively *de novo*; it is frankly literal, as objective as possible, and seeks to embrace the total verbality of the poem. Where tempted into the bypaths of exegesis it has tried to shun the excesses of Alexandria and to preserve the intended letter. For its justification we turn to Eliot's ascertainable position on words and their uses.

No concern is more pervasive throughout Eliot's developmentally consistent forty years of critical writing than his urgent sense of the writer's responsibility toward his language:

> Every writer who does not help to develop the language is to the extent to which he is read a positive agent of deterioration.[3]

> It is the business of the writer as artist to preserve the beauty and precision of the language.[4]

> Every great writer contributes something to the meaning of the key words which he uses.[5]

Eliot praises one who "thinks structurally and respects the meaning of words,"[6] and censures the "irresponsibility towards the meaning of words [which] is not infrequent"[7] as in the case of the author of *The Raven* who "in his choice of the word which has the right *sound* ... is by no means careful that it should have also the right sense. "[8] If "Crashaw is, in fact, among our minor poets, because decoration distracts him,"[9] and if the "beautiful line for its own sake is a luxury dangerous even for the poet who has made himself a virtuoso of the technique of the theatre,"[10] we have a reason for the deliberately spare vocabulary of the *Quartets*—taken apart its everydayness would belie the strange effectiveness of its compounding—which prefers "direct suggestiveness by precise reference" to the "meretricious suggestiveness of vague literary association."[11]

The number of quotable and revealing comments specifically directed at matters of vocabulary would make a sizable collection of precepts confirmed by example in Eliot's poetic practice. Singled out for admiration are immediacy and particularity,[12] compression, austerity, lucidity, aptness—all qualities making for "ordonnance and precision." Warning is sounded against devitalization by loss of contact with things and emotions,[13] and the artificial dichotomy of poetic versus prose diction deplored. An interesting point made in this connection is that while we are ready enough to accept a classification of "poetic prose," we "appear to have overlooked the right of poetry to be 'prosaic.' "[14] Thus, as early as 1921 Eliot's discussion of the structural possibilities of the long poem indicates the lines of his own development of them. His recognition of the inevitability of shifting levels of intensity and the consequent need of alternate tension and relaxation fits in with his conception of such a poem as a vehicle of highly complex states of awareness.[15] Although bracketing psychology with aesthetics as one of "the two most dangerous subjects of study for the poet,"[16] Eliot makes unerring application of its findings on the resolution by linear exposition of conflicts arising from the very simultaneity of potentially incompatible attitudes.[17] The ordering of experience which is an implicit aim of all art is a conscious objective of the *Quartets* and is sought most delicately and without oversimplification in the successive evocations of mood and thought which draw exhaustively on the "feelings inhering...in particular words or phrases or images."[18] Much of the weight which is not that of statement is carried by "the music of verse [which] is inseparable from the meanings and associations of words"[19] and by the rhythm envisioned as a "quality...which no system of scansion can define," "a highly personal matter.... the scheme of organization of thought, feeling, and vocabulary, the way in which everything comes together."[20]

This verbal organization, always a prime consideration, is of peculiar moment in poetry, whose structural differences from prose Eliot signalizes in a letter to the editor of the *Times Literary Supplement* commenting on the leading article (called "Questions of Prose") of a previous issue[21] in which the writer had called Shakespeare's Coriolanus' speech "better prose" than North's Plutarch's. Shakespeare's version, Eliot objects, is good verse and bad prose: its word order and emphases are those of verse, for "verse, whatever else it may or may not be, is itself a system of *punctuation*; the usual marks of punctuation are differently employed."[22] (That this last assumption underlies Eliot's own usage is abundantly evident, and awareness of it legitimates many seeming liberties.[23])

Eliot's whole approach to syntax appears to be based upon the primacy of the word—not words fitted into an existing pattern, but determining their own pattern by intrinsic necessity. With him it is, as with Marianne Moore in the review already quoted, a case of "conscious and complete appreciation of every word, and in relation to every other word, as it goes by."[24] But there must be "no single word or phrase which calls too much attention to itself, or which is not there for the sake of the total effect....[25] In finding this and kindred qualities to praise in Kipling, Eliot goes on to contrast the balladist's methods and attitudes with his own in an unexpected bit of self-disclosure, and hints at something prior even to the word. For some, "the poem may begin to shape itself in fragments of musical rhythm, and its structure will first appear in terms of something analogous to musical form....."[26] This hint is developed more fully in *The Music of Poetry,* his most explicit formulation of a poetic and prosodic credo, and required reading for a student of the *Quartets* as the composition having the closest musical affinities of his entire repertoire. This aspect has been so masterfully treated by Miss Helen Gardner[27] as to render further discussion futile. Suffice it to note that on Eliot's own testimony the broader musical organization is conscious and deliberate; in keeping with this intention is the characteristic structural device of the repeated and modulated short phrase whose appearance in new contexts resembles the thematic development and return within a movement of a symphony. Would it be fantastic to envisage a "translation" for orchestra of, say, *The Dry Salvages*, not as program music, but with a genuine equivalence of relation (a ratio once being arbitrarily set) between structural units or groupings?

One readily concurs in the attribution to Eliot of powers of auditory imagination more highly developed than those of the visual (without implying the defect of the visual which Eliot scathes in Milton[28]) as made by Miss Gardner[29] as well as by a student[30] of the French influences on his early poetic growth. This hypersensitivity to sound values exteriorizes itself in rhythms and cadences and exploitation of timbres where a visual poet (Gautier is selected for comparison) would seek expression in forms and contours and a different type of imagery.

His early recognized "distinctive cadence... [and] personal modus of arrangement"[31] have always been conceived in terms of a greater and organic whole functioning through the perfect articulation of its members. Every ligament and tendon is there for the purpose of being called into play to facilitate the fluid verbal adjustments of his athletic verse. The question of syntax arises in most of Eliot's reviews of newer works and is a measuring rod for the old as well. Of Denham's *Cooper's Hill* he writes: "The structure of the poem deserves admiration, and also the precision of syntax which makes tolerable the faded vocabulary."[32] And to him "every battle [Mallarmé] fought with syntax represents the effort to transmute lead into gold, ordinary language into poetry...."[33]

"Ordinary language," contemporary idiom, must be earth to the poetic Atlas and must be tapped for the infusion of vigor constantly needed "to stimulate the worn nerves and release the arthritic limbs of our diction."[34] On the other hand, "If rhetoric is any convention of writing inappropriately applied, this conversational style can and does become a rhetoric.... Much of the second and third rate in American *vers libre* is of this sort; and much of the second and third rate in English Wordsworthianism. There is in fact no conversational or other form which can be applied indiscriminately...."[35]

Although Eliot in many passages seems to equate "rhetoric" with bombast or affectation he suggests re-examination of the term and a greater precision in its application: "We begin to suspect that the word is merely a vague term of abuse for any style that is bad.... It is one of those words which it is the business of criticism to dissect and reassemble. Let us void the assumption that rhetoric is a vice of manner, and endeavor to find a rhetoric of substance also, which is right because it issues from what it has to express."[36]

What is referred to in the title of this paper as Eliot's rhetoric is "skillful or artistic use of speech," not "artificial elegance of language" (Webster), and is close to the idea of the classical and medieval discipline whose "colors," figures of thought and figures of speech, have their very real counterparts in the composition under discussion.

We can, with reservations, say of Eliot what he says of his "Metaphysical Poets:" "The language... is as a rule simple and pure.... The structure of the sentences, on the other hand, is sometimes far from simple, but this is not a vice; it is a fidelity to thought amd feeling."[37]

This fidelity is the answer to most technical questions prompted by the protean *Quartets,* which represent the culmination of a craftsman's efforts[38] as well as the proliferation and fulfilment of much that was merely germinal in his less mature poetic thought.[39]

After a prudent hint that "it is time for a reminder that the music of verse is not a line by line matter, but a question of the whole poem"[40] this introductory chapter can be concluded with two further cautions, which, however, bear out the use to which we have put Eliot's prose remarks, viz., to illuminate his own ripest poetic practice.

The poet, when he talks or writes about poetry, has peculiar qualifications and peculiar limitations: if we allow for the latter we can better appreciate the former—a caution which I recommend to poets themselves as well as to the readers of what they say about poetry. I can never read any of my own prose writings without acute embarrassment: I shirk the task, and consequently may not take account of all the assertions to which I have at one time or another committed myself; I may often repeat what I have said before, and I may equally well contradict myself. But I believe that the critical writings of poets, of which in the past there have been some very distinguished examples, owe a great deal of their interest to the fact that at the back of the poet's mind, if not as his ostensible purpose, he is always trying to defend the kind of poetry he is writing, or to formulate the kind that he wants to write.[41]

Poets, when they meditate about poetry at all, are liable to generalize either from their own accomplishment or from their own designs; and their purposes and interests, if more exact, may also be narrower than those of their readers, so that their pronouncements should usually be considered in relation to their own poems. What the poet has to say about poetry, will often be most valuable when it consists of introspective observation of his own processes.[42]

🌿 1 🌿

Burnt Norton

THE OPENING LINES of the first section of Burnt Norton:[1]

1 Time present and time past
2 Are both perhaps present in time future
3 And time future contained in time past

appropriately constitute a thematic statement (in the musical sense) of the interrelations of time past, present and future which are to recur as motives throughout the *Four Quartets*. Both the thought pattern[2] and the rhetorical pattern with their reiterated "time" in stressed positions impart a gnomic quality which colors the immediately succeeding pair of "plain" sentences:

4 If all time is eternally present
5 All time is unredeemable.
6 What might have been is an abstraction
7 Remaining a perpetual possibility
8 Only in a world of speculation.

After this the dissolving spell is caught up again in

9 What might have been and what has been
10 Point to one end, which is always present

before its concretization in the garden imagery which follows (lines 11 ff.).

The effect of 1-3 resides partly in the position of the adjectives as well as in their interplay. The departure from normal word order in each of the five occurrences of the attributives with the chime-like identical noun sets the passage apart from ordinary discourse. Unique and unitary, it has a strong line-to-line linkage that becomes characteristic

1

of verse series similar in tone.[3] The predicate "present" in line 2 binds while it varies, and the juxtaposed "in time future,/And time future" creates an impression of the incremental repetition of folk charm or nursery tale. The simplicity and assurance proper to these are however vitiated by the rather central "perhaps" which communicates an air of tentativeness extended even to the participle "contained" which it may be considered as also modifying. The absence of a finite verb in line 3 increases its dependence on the foregoing, and the concluding "in time past" completes the internal reference and closes the unit with double decisiveness, by the finality of the word "past" as contrasted with an uncircumscribed "future," and by the simultaneously chiastic and parallel figure it fills:

> and...past   and...future
> in...future   in...past

The verbal tension is further heightened by exhausting the (mathematical) combination of the three words, "present," "past," and "future":

> 1 present...past
> 2 present...future
> 3 future...past

Seen thus in isolation the words tend to assume the trappings of a syllogism, or at least to imply that "things equal to the same thing are equal to each other." (And line 4 makes this explicit.)

Another quasi-mathematical relationship is suggested by the medial and initial "and's" in lines 1 and 3 respectively:

> 1 present   *and*   past
> 2   present-future
> 3 *and* future-past

It is as though a proportion were being set up between the halves of line 1 and the 2nd and 3rd lines:

> present : past : : present-future : future-past

Similarly, the term "future" appears to be the mean proportional between "present" and "past." This last is an arresting consideration as indicating the transcendence of logic and chronology which would read "present" as the middle term between "past" and "future." Syntactically there is no such violation; the sense might be reasonably reduced to "Past and present determine future," which would indeed be "unredeemable" in terms of the deterministic view from which the implied "Redeem the time" preserves us. The spatial configuration of the words can be seen therefore as counterpointing the grammatical and adding to the complexity of the latter a (wholesomely) disturbing element of the non-discursive.

The solemnity of the utterance is enhanced by the relatively unslurrable labials and dentals which dominate the consonant composition of the three lines, where no liquid but the almost entirely inconspicuous "r" eases transitions. The vowels are well hemmed in—the only open syllable is the first in "future." The wide vowel range of the second line emphasizes by contrast the restricted scope of the lines preceding and following.

All this may seeem an excessively tortuous reading of a fairly straightforward and very brief passage. But Eliot has on more than one occasion granted *carte blanche* to would-be explicators of poetic texts. For example: "It is a commonplace to observe that the meaning of a poem may wholly escape paraphrase. It is not quite so commonplace to observe that the meaning of a poem may be something larger than its author's conscious purpose, and something remote from its origins."[4] Particularly applicable to the poem under discussion are the following remarks made in a 1951 B.B.C. broadcast with reference to Vergil's fourth *Eclogue:*

> If a prophet were by definition a man who understood the full meaning of what he was saying, this would be for me the end of the matter [viz., that Vergil's conscious concern was only with domestic affairs and Roman politics]. But if the word "inspiration" is to have any meaning, it must mean just this, that the speaker or writer is uttering something which he does not wholly understand—or which he may even misinterpret when the inspiration has departed from him. This is certainly true of poetic inspiration: and there is still better reason for admiring Isaiah as a poet than for claiming Vergil as a prophet. A poet may believe that he is expressing only his private experience; his lines may be for him only a means of talking about himself without giving himself away; yet for

his readers what he has written may come to be the expression both of their own secret feelings and of the
exultation or despair of a generation.[5]

To return to *Burnt Norton*—the terse statement of lines 4
and 5,

> If all time is eternally present
> All time is unredeemable.

neat clause per neat line, relieves its monosyllables in the
contrasting second half-lines which complete the matching
first. The hint of question-and-answer in condition and
apodosis is strengthened by repeating, catechism-wise, "All
time is" a trifle more slowly than on its appearance a moment
ago with the introductory "If." We are inclined to give the
same temporal value to both lines, retarding the second ever
so slightly (or lengthening "All" and "un-") to compensate for
the syllable missing at either end (as compared with the
count above). The hemistichal four-stress character of these
lines confims the beat felt in "Time present and time past"
(line 1) but weakened in the interim lines. This rhythmic
matrix is perceived with varying intensity throughout the
section to which it is basic much as the heartbeat fades and
loudens under shifting stress. Its underlying presence gives
cohesiveness and imposes a certain restraint within which
ingenuity is exercised to secure the differentiated tonal
effects which are realized in terms of line length and weight,
position and number of unstressed elements, the placing or
neglecting of the caesura, and other factors depending on the
sounds of the component words as these are conditioned by
the sense and connotation.

Thus the end-stopped quality of lines 1-5 is altered in the
next group of three lines which but for the typography
would be read in one breath:

> 6 What might have been is an abstraction
> 7 Remaining a perpetual possibility
> 8 Only in a world of speculation.

The main stresses are accordingly muted and internal pauses
unapparent. These become deliberate again only as we
approach the remembered garden with its echoing footfalls.

Yet in each of these lines as in those preceding the last

word assumes a dominance and key-relation to what goes before:

> Past - future - past - present
> unredeemable - abstraction - possibility - speculation

Viewed from this position a new four-four alignment asserts itself beneath the three-two-three syntactical pattern as a second instance of the species of counterpoint noted above.[6]

The crisp precision of 6-8 arises chiefly from the diction. Although line 6 shows the monosyllabic first half plus copula plus polysyllable pattern of lines 4 and 5 there is a difference in rhythm, a lightening brought about by the quickly spoken "What might have been" with its single strong stress balancing "is an abstraction." Economy of phrase replaces phrasal echo in the pregnant sentence which, admitting the real limitations of "a world of speculation," recognizes also its imaginative force as a modifier of experience. The alliterated "perpetual possibility" with the participle binding it more intimately than would a clause to the "abstraction" which has been equated with "what might have been" keeps up the rhythmic impression of a rapidly turning wheel which is continued in the next line and which in both depends on the suppression of one of the four beats and the even disposition of the three remaining. "Only" gains emphasis by recalling the accent to the first syllable of the line as in 1 and 5 and by its apt situation in the sentence.

Lines 9 and 10:

> 9 What might have been and what has been
> 10 Point to one end, which is always present.

tie up by repetition, "What might have been," and by paraphrase, "what has been," the double thread of the theme as originally stated and as modulated. Again we find the significant initial stress, "Point," which, as hitherto, marks its line as opening or closing a thought unit. The "one end, which is always present" is so in a deeper sense than was mere "time" above, since we are speaking of the potential (but not future) as well as the actual. Have we here something of the "presence" Gabriel Marcel describes in *Mystery of Being*?[7] As always, the layered meanings offer shifting faces. Like sliding planes of graphite in comparison with other crystals having marked lines of cleavage they yield more to microscopic analysis than under the geologist's hammer.

In the next verses we move out of the philosophical realm into the psychological, and thence into the projected garden itself. 11-14 are transcribed here with spaces between the halflines to suggest the experiment of reading down the four first halves as if they were continuous:

> 11 Footfalls echo   in the memory
> 12 Down the passage   which we did not take
> 13 Towards the door   we never opened
> 14 Into the rose-garden.[8]...

Again it is pattern more than statement which conveys the underlying tension between wish-fulfilment and frustration. We are teased into regarding "Footfalls echo down the passage towards the door into the rose-garden" as climactic fact, ignoring the mounting force of the denials until we are brought up short with

> 14 .... My words echo
> 15 Thus, in your mind.

The recall to reality is complete. The unnoticed personal pronoun "we" becomes suddenly specific in the possessives "My" and "your." The incomplete line increases the finality. The parallel of "My words echo" to "Footfalls echo" implies a correspondence of "in your mind" to "in the memory" and to the latter phrase's expansion in the next two and a half lines. "Thus [comma]," carrying strong stress and duplicating the urgency of "Down the," "Towards the," "Into," is a triumph of compression and a hint of the second pervasive theme of the poem, that of the problem of communication.

The next three lines (we have numbered them as distinct lines because of their typographical arrangement) are set apart in a kind of visual isolation:

> 16   But to what purpose
> 17 Disturbing the dust on a bowl of rose-leaves
> 18 I do not know.

They seem parenthetic rather than transitional.[9]

Their deliberately faulty syntax gives rise to a healthy

crop of ambiguities centering on the function of "Disturb-ing." A first reading takes it as a gerund, implicitly correcting the sentence to something like "But what is the purpose of disturbing...I do not know," which seems to express the futility of stirring up buried memories. Another possibility ignores the break with the preceding sentence, refers the clause "to what purpose...I do not know" to "echo...in your mind," and sees "Disturbing" as a participle modifying "My words." The absence of line-end commas does not militate against this interpretation[10] but the yoking of images it enforces—the bowl of rose-leaves in the mind—would be less metaphysical than merely inept, and leads us to reject as jejune such a reading and to prefer the unjustified gerund. We may however assign a double role to "But to what purpose" and let it remain a tacit comment on the sentence before it at the same time as it relates to "Disturbing...."

The sound-links are subtle. Paired assonances in stressed syllables of adjacent feet, a device broached above in "Towards the door" (line 13), occur in "purpose / Disturbing" and "bowl of rose-." The abbreviated line 18 reproduces singly the d-d plus o-o sound-shape of 17:

disturbing-dust   bowl-rose
    do   know

We are tempted to mention counterpoint again in the mirroring of "words.../Thus" (14/15) in "Disturbing... dust." A final glance at these lines leaves us wondering why it is "*My* words and "*your* mind" rather than the reverse, and whether the "dist-...dust" combination is intentional.

With line 19 we move into the quick-phrased, half-believed, half-experienced atmosphere charged with verbal reminiscence[11] and highly personal import—the multiple power of the "x" in this equation renders it susceptible of many values.

19   Other echoes
20 Inhabit the garden. Shall we follow?
21 Quick, said the bird, find them, find them,
22 Round the corner. Through the first gate,
23 Into our first world, shall we follow
24 The deception of the thrush? Into our first world.

The effect of enchantment is fostered by the personification of the "Other echoes" (or, less compelling, their employment in synecdoche) and the blending of the concrete and abstract in "Through the first gate,/Into our first world." The participation of the reader is ensured by the repeated invitation "Shall we follow?"—the objects (of "follow") fuse the echoes with the thrush's call; the destination is more state than place. One recalls just such a deserted formal garden whose alleys and terraces and elusive and insistent thrush seemed to transport one miles and years from actuality into a sort of Midsummer's Eve spell. "Deception" is a telling word in the face of this illusion.[12] The passage from action to reflection is almost instantaneous, from the bird's imperatives to the second "Into our first world" punctuated as a complete sentence in its meditative repetition of the phrase which in the line above has linked the two modes of experience. Following close upon "find them, find them,/Round the corner [period]," the capitalized "Through the first gate" and its parallel "Into our first world" seem to belong to both the hurried directions and the hesitant acceptance. This double-duty syntax is an old device,[13] but here it works by insinuation rather than by challenge.

The tense usage is interesting in the light of the opening lines which asserted the present-ness of all time. "Shall we follow?" is less future tense than present intention, but "said the bird" is a genuine shift, anticipating the consistent past of the largest portion of section I which follows—as far as the last "said the bird" which leads back to (present) considerations of time past and future and ends on a repetition of lines 9 and 10, a fitting refrain to terminate the first of the five formal divisions of the *Quartet.*

The "they" passages (11. 25-31 and 32-41) exhibit a progression in two phases to a climax of realization, then a rapid dénouement.

> 25 There they were, dignified, invisible,
> 26 Moving without pressure, over the dead leaves,
> 27 In the autumn heat, through the vibrant air,
> 28 And the bird called, in response to
> 29 The unheard music hidden in the shrubbery,
> 30 And the unseen eyebeam crossed, for the roses
> 31 Had the look of flowers that are looked at.

The focal phrases are "There they were" (11. 25 and 32), introducing either step, and "And they were" (1. 40), at the peak. The succession is from perception via external objects (the bird, the roses) to a somewhat more immediate awareness ("behind us, reflected in the pool").

32 There they were as our guests, accepted and accepting.
33 So we moved, and they, in a formal pattern,
34 Along the empty alley, into the box circle,
35 To look down into the drained pool.
36 Dry the pool, dry concrete, brown edged,
37 And the pool was filled with water out of sunlight,
38 And the lotos rose, quietly, quietly,
39 The surface glittered out of heart of light,
40 And they were behind us, reflected in the pool.
41 Then a cloud passed, and the pool was empty

The echoes, or the sources of the echoes, "they," may perhaps be most satisfactorily referred to as "presences."[14] "Invisible," "unheard," "hidden," "unseen" describe their first manifestations, sensed (although extra-sensorily[15]) in 25-27, recognized in the responses attributed to the bird (28-29) and to the conscious roses (30-31). But once "accepted and accepting" they accompany our steps, "dignified" (25), "in a formal pattern" (33), through the second set of negating adjectives, "empty," "drained," "dry" (34, 35, 36) to the mirage of 37-39. Line 40 gives the illusory fulfillment of "what might have been," line 41, "what has been." There is a kinship of feeling here with Barrie's *Dear Brutus*, but the whole can be taken quite simply as record, not allegory.[16] The hint of negative purification (a third and very important theme of the *Quartets*) will be developed more explicitly in section III of *Burnt Norton* as well as later in *East Coker* III, *The Dry Salvages* III and *Little Gidding passim*.

There are more phrasal parallels which strengthen the correspondence between the two blocks of verses.[17] After each "There they were" we find the double modifier, with amplification in 32 by means of the appositional "as our guests" and the conjunction between the participles. "Moving without pressure" (26(matches "So we moved, and they" (32); again the second member is amplified, here with the

added subject pronoun. Three prepositional phrases modify
the form of "move" in 26 and 32 and occupy the same line
positions (the second half of 26 and 32, both halves of 27 and
34); in the second trio a disyllabic noun replaces each
monosyllable of the first, wile the adjectives are identical in
syllable count but mirror-fashion: dead—autumn—vibrant,
formal—empty—box. The "pool" lines (35-41) represent a
lengthy insert with its own internal *amplificatio* in the
repeated "pool" (the word occurs in five of the seven lines),
"dry," "and the," "quietly," before the bird is readmitted:

    42 Go, said the bird; for the leaves were full of children
    43 Hidden excitedly, containing laughter.
    44 Go, go, go, said the bird: human kind
    45 Cannot bear very much reality.

This time the hidden music in the shrubbery is revealed as
children's laughter, still unheard because contained (29, 42-
43). And human kind must go, abashed by the unseen
eyebeam (30, 44-45). Deeper than irony is the recommended
flight from the reality of intense inter-personal experience
("My words," "your mind," "the door we never opened").

   "Go, said the bird" (42 and 44) also closes the inner
envelope that "Quick, said the bird" (21) began. After it
comes the summary already remarked:[18]

    46 Time past and time future
    47 What might have been and what has been
    48 Point to one end, which is always present.

46 varies, 47-48 duplicate 1 and 9-10 and the circle is
complete.

   The individual word-play is here less significant that the
manipulation of larger units. 31 and 32 give us "look" (noun)
and "looked at," "accepted and accepting," but these pairs are
not the elaborate "Andrewisms" Eliot uses elsewhere[19] in
imitation of his favorite preacher. Sound suits sense in 36ff.
where "dry concrete, brown edged" diminishes the full
quality of "pool" not wanted until the contrasting "pool was
filled." In the next line "lotos rose" gives a vowel richness
carried on in the two "quietly's"—this would have been lost
had the more facile "lily" (jingling with filled") been employed
for the water-plant in question. The spelling in "-os" recalls

the fruit and its legend and so deepens the connotative complexity.

Section II of *Burnt Norton* is subdivided into three metrically distinct portions; fifteen irregularly rhymed octosyllabics, eight long lines which appear to have six stresses and strong caesural pauses (four are marked by full stops, one each by colon and semi-colon, two by commas), and twenty-one "normal" lines (the free four-stress type of section I and the bulk of the poem) arranged in two verse paragraphs of thirteen and eight lines respectively.

The arresting vocabulary of the "Garlic and sapphires" passage—these few lines show a higher percentage than any comparable selection from elsewhere in the *Quartets* of words occurring nowhere else in the poem—calls attention to the microcosm-macrocosm character of the imagery in which all material orders of being are represented—animal, vegetable and mineral, terrestrial and sidereal—in a kind of compenetration analogous to the simultaneity of all time which section I has pressed. The syntax, too, though simple, startles.

49 Garlic and sapphires in the mud
50 Clot the bedded axle-tree.

It is not the mud, but the garlic and sapphires which prevent the wheel from turning.

51 The trilling wire in the blood
52 Sings below inveterate scars
53 And reconciles forgotten wars.

The wars which are reconciled are the forgotten ones.

54 The dance along the artery
55 The circulation of the lymph
56 Are figured in the drift of stars
57 Ascend to summer in the tree

The expected period does not close line 57 although we are prompted to end the sentence here because of the symmetry so satisfied. The four-line unit (entirely unpunctuated)[20] runs: subject, subject, predicate, predicate. The last six lines are clearly a single sentence and show a measure of subordination which contrasts with the parataxis of the first nine:

58 We move above the moving tree
59 In light upon the figured leaf
60 And hear upon the sodden floor
61 Below, the boarhound and the boar
62 Pursue their pattern as before
63 But reconciled among the stars.

The monotony which we must assume to be intended is hardly relieved by the inversion of the first foot in 49 ("Garlic") and the omission of the initial slack syllable in 50 ("Clot") and 52 ("Sings"), and is all the more pronounced by reason of the unusual uniformity of line structure—eleven of the fifteen end in prepositional phrases, in only three of which the noun has a modifier—"moving" (58), "figured" (59), "sodden" (60)—between it and the definite article, while in only two is there either further modification—"in the drift of stars" (56)—or absence of the article—"below inveterate scars" (52). It is interesting to note that all the adjectives here are participles—"bedded" (50), "trilling" (51), "forgotten" (53), "reconciled" (63), the three already enumerated, and even "inveterate" (52) if its Latin derivation in -*atus* be taken into account. The effect of compression this produces is not dissipated so much as complemented by the peculiar expansion simulated by the (inexact) repetition at some distance of certain words not otherwise signalized: "-tree" (50) and "tree" (57 and 58), "reconciles" (53) and "reconciled" (63), "Are figured" (56) and "figured leaf" (59), "stars" (56 and 63). At closer intervals there are "move" and "moving" (58), "boarhound" and "boar" (61).

The disposition of the rhymes in 49-63 is somewhat curious. Although nothing in the preceding section has prepared us for the new rhythm, we are sufficiently caught up by the first three lines, " . . . mud," " . . . tree," " . . . blood," to want to close the fancied quatrain with a second b-rhyme, and the disappointment of this expectation brings a peculiar reminder of Emily Dickinson, between whom and Eliot we should claim few affinities. The delayed rhyme, "-tree" (50) - "artery" (54), echoed in the identical "tree" (57 and 58), the recurrent (and concluding) rhyme on "stars" (admitting the eye-rhyme "wars" [53]), the triple rhyme "floor," "boar," "before" (60-62), the possible pairing of "lymph" (55) with "leaf" (59), impress us as somehow functional and not merely decorative. So do the subtler alliteration (perhaps more suitably termed consonant-chime because of its occurrence in other than initial positions), internal half-rhyme and assonance. Within lines we may cite "circulation...*l*ymph" (55), "*fig*ured...d*rif*t" (56), "A*sc*end...*s*ummer" (57), "*mov*e ab*ov*e" (58). Between lines we find such linkages as "*m*ud"-"bed-" (49-50), "*Cl*ot"-"*bl*ood" (50-51), "-*ing*"-"*Sings*" (51-52), "inveter*ate*"-"*re*conciles" (52-53), "*reconciles*"-"*d*ance *a*long" (53-54), "*B*elow"-"*be*fore" (61-62). In three of the last examples the members alternate in stress, the first and weaker element making itself felt only as a sympathetic vibration when the second note is struck, or as something one half remembers hearing before.

There are two sound-threads running through the entire passage, vowel-plus-liquid (and the reverse) and vowel-plus-nasal; the favored consonants "r" and "n," with all possible vowel accompaniment in close chromatic variation and changing degrees of intensity comparable to those produced by reinforcement and interference of similarly pitched sound waves of different amplitudes. One could refine indefinitely on these relationships and their complications such as "sapph*ires*"-"*wire*" (49 and 51), "*in* the *bl*ood"-"*below in-*" (51 and 52), "sodden"-"pattern" (60 and 62). Although the sound and letter play recalls the Welsh devices exploited by Hopkins this effect is muted. The overall texture is nervous and closely knit, its integrity depending on interrelations resembling the chemist's conception of bonding in a giant molecule of some organic compound.

The movement of the eight-line "turning world" passage which comes next may be appropriately described as rotary.

64   At[21] the still point of the turning world. Neither flesh nor fleshless;

65   Neither from nor towards; at the still point, there the dance is,

66   But neither arrest nor movement. And do not call it fixity,

67   Where past and future are gathered. Neither movement from nor towards,

68   Neither ascent nor decline. Except for the point, the still point,

69 There would be no dance, and there is only the
dance.
70 I can only say, *there* we have been: but I cannot say
where.
71 And I cannot say, how long, for that is to place it in
time.

The balanced half-lines—and many of the halves fall into
halves again—the neither-nor pairs, the repetitions of phrase
and word, circle round the non-dimensional, non-temporal
"still point" of intensely realized experience, be it of
communion or simple awareness. The clustered negatives—
there are nine, counting each neither-nor combination as a
single instance, in the eight-line span—and the near-
negatives "except" and "only" (twice) deepen the furrow
traced by the "empty," "drained," "dry" lines (34ff.) of the
preceding section and reaffirm the ineffable "presence" that
was its burden—"And do not call it fixity." The circuit is
increasingly centripetal, the central "still point" being
temporally between past and future, locally between from
and towards, ascent, and decline (note the two planes,
although on each the envisaged motion is strictly linear), in
state between arrest and movement, in nature between flesh
and fleshless. All these attributes are expressed as syntactical
absolutes, with only the loosest of implied predication of
"point" or "dance." Instead of adding up to zero they seem
rather a stripping of limitations from the very positive dance.
This key term relates to earlier passages, the movement "in a
formal pattern" of line 33, the "dance along the artery" of
line 54, and anticipates later development as in the first
section of *East Coker*. The dependence of this dance upon its
hub or fulcrum, the "still point" of its perpetual reference, is
complete. Poised between semantic contradictories, it must
transcend them. Einstein's dimensional categories having
been exhausted, we are left with what can only be spiritual
reality. The wording, however, is still exploratory. We
progress from expletive "there" (69) to adverb "there" (70),
but the certainty is intuitive rather than ratiocinative.
Nothing now impedes the turning wheel, and the interest is
no longer peripheral or cosmic, but literally concentrated in
the new mode of apprehension imaged in the dance with its

connotations of order and ritual and emotive significance. If the "we" in line 58, "We move above the moving tree," indicates shared experience, and "I can only say...I cannot say....I cannot say" is reminiscent of Jeremias at the beginning of his vocation as prophet. Although one hesitates to use the much abused term "mystical," there is scope for it (at least as a strongly suggested analogue[22] for aesthetic experience) here and wherever in the *Quartets* Eliot seeks to give expression to essentially incommunicable experience known in its depth rather than its scene, its intensity rather than its duration.

In the longest portion of section II, the first nine lines attack the same problem descriptively:

72   The inner freedom from the practical desire,
73 The release from action and suffering, release from the inner
74 And the outer compulsion, yet surrounded
75 By a grace of sense, a white light still and moving,
76 *Erhebung* without motion, concentration
77 Without elimination, both a new world
78 And the old made explicit, understood
79 In the completion of its partial ecstasy,
80 The resolution of its partial horror.

The final period may be said to close the attempt to find less inadequate language; we have had a series of substantives variously qualified, but no finite verb. There is an urgency in the phrasing, with each major constuction tried again before its abandonment for another (three with "from" in 72-73, two with "without" in 76-77, two with "of" in 79-80). In the vocabulary the groping is more apparent, as is seen in appositives nearly synonymous ("freedom" and "release"), opposites joined with "and" (still in the negative role in which they were cast above—64-71), the shift from abstract to concrete (in line 75) and back, the necessity of supplying something (the protagonist?) for "surrounded" (74) to modify. We notice an elasticity in the grouping of parallels: there is an implied equivalence of "practical desire" (72), "action and suffering" (73) and "the inner / And the outer compulsion" (73-74). (In the last phrase the definite article is omitted before the now generalized "release" and inserted

where it is with a marked effect of particularity.) A nice
tension is set up between the "inner freedom" and the "inner
compulsion" which are spatially balanced rather than
syntactically opposed. Quiescence and relief are only part of
the picture. Response is manifested by the upward tendency
("*Erhebung*," 76) which accompanies the sensible consolation
felt as the "white light."

Except for "ecstasy" (79) and "horror" (80) (both,
however, only "partial") the diction of this passage with its
Latinate -tion words might be characterized as prosaic,
almost legalistic. But as Eliot himself observes of the larger
whole of St.-John Perse's *Anabase,* "[i] ts sequences, its logic
of imagery are those of poetry and not of prose; and in
consequence—at least the two matters are very closely
allied—the *declamation,* the system of stresses and pauses,
which is partially exhibited by the punctuation and spacing, is
that of poetry and not of prose."[23]

Lines 81-84 return to orthodox sentence structure,[24]
compact with maximum participial means to economy of
language and with nouns making the most of more than one
part of speech.

    81 Yet the enchainment of past and future
    82 Woven in the weakness of the changing body,
    83 Protects mankind from heaven and damnation
    84 Which flesh cannot endure.

"Enchainment" (81) and "damnation" (83) denote the result
of verbal action, "past," "future" (81) and "weakness" (82) are
adjectival in origin. The matter-of-fact phrasing suits the
idea of being brought back (with some relief—"protects") to
material reality, and the rather large proportion of Anglo-
Saxon words ("yet," "woven," "weakness," "body," "mankind," "heaven," "flesh") increases, at least to our prepossess-
sions regarding etymological tonality, the feeling of
earthiness.

The transition to the final argumentative reflection of
section II is signalized by the typographical break between
lines 84 and 85. These are spaced as complementary half-
lines, with the effect of telescoping the full stress-span of
their counterparts near the close of section I:

human kind
45   Cannot bear very much reality.
46 Time past and time future

The later lines

84   Which flesh cannot endure.
85   Time past and time future

are actually more amplification than echo, as their immediate context makes apparent.

The opening statement

85   Time past and time future
86 Allow but a little consciousness.

is taken up almost syllogistically by

87 To be conscious is not to be in time
88   But only in time...

which, while it does not really define, certainly limits the meaning of "consciousness" to the type of acute awareness which has so far defied accurate description. Taking the absence of punctuation after line 87 as the special verse usage Eliot allows[25]—the term "poetic license" is in fact if not in flavor quite admissible—we may begin a new sentence, and a more fully developed thought (note that the tangible experiences remembered serve to give substance to the otherwise—and elsewhere—tentative claim) with its paradoxical conclusion:

88 But only in time can the moment in the rose-garden
89 The moment in the arbour where the rain beat,
90 The moment in the draughty church at smokefall
91 Be remembered; involved with past and future.
92 Only through time time is conquered.

On the strength of our appreciation of the garden encounter of section I we are trusted to give due value to the vignettes[26] of the arbor and the church (both images stress the insecurity of the shelter they afford—perhaps as part of the underlying ascesis). If "arbour" and "church" are respectively paralleled by "past" and "future," and if the arbor justly recalls the hyacinth garden of *The Waste Land* I,[27] are we dealing, even collaterally, with fall and reparation, or

failure and new purpose?[28] The change of weather and of
time of day separate the experiences of rose-garden, arbor
and church even if the first two are locally the same. Of the
three, only the garden has been emphatically linked with
"time present," but with this as an all-inclusive tense suiting
the quasi-infinite breadth of the experience. Its familiarity
renders unnecessary the characterizing modifiers of the
newly introduced arbor—and church-moments. The elements of wind and rain and the pregnant coinage "smokefall"
prepare us indirectly for the four-element theme that is to be
of major significance as the poem develops. There is even an
echo of "the winds blew and the floods came...," and what
happened to the house we see in *East Coker.*

The pithy closing line of section II, "Only through time
time is conquered" (92), representing not so much capitulation to the inevitable as grasp of the limitations of created
nature, sums up in its perfect symmetry the means-and-end
adjustment that has been the problem so far. The emphasis
falls on the repeated key word, which tends in each half-line
to assume the length and weight of the combination of
syllables completing each. The pattern is

2 syllables 1 syllable time time   1 syllable 2 syllables.

Section III opens with a nine-line sentence of peculiar
structure:

93 Here is a place of disaffection
94 Time before and time after
95 In a dim light: neither daylight
96 Investing form with lucid stillness
97 Turning shadow into transient beauty
98 With slow rotation suggesting permenence
99 Nor darkness to purify the soul
100 Emptying the sensual with deprivation
101 Cleansing affection from the temporal.

We are at first struck by the seemingly incompatible
appositives "place" (93) and "time" (94), but with division into
lines as sole "punctuation" and simple juxtaposition affording
scant clue to their real relationship we may read 93-94 as an
agglomerative predication clothing the (material) present,
"Here" (93), with its accidents of place and quality ("of

disaffection"), time and relation ("before" and "after"). The adverbs shade into other parts of speech with increasingly concrete effect. "Here" is pronominal with the force of *hic* in Latin: "before" and "after" replace the now familiar "past" and "future," and the aura of remoteness is dispelled by their tendency to slip into prepositional roles, implying the tangible chronology of "before" one datable event and "after" another and therefore within precise limits of quotidian experience. Among the meanings assignable to "disaffection" (93)—alienation, disloyalty, disgust, discontent, (physical) indisposition, and the various opposites of "affection" taken as a) the affective in general, b) attribute or property, c) alterable condition or accident[29]—we are not forced to any rigorous exclusion but guided in possible and shifting choices by the phrasal development as the sentence accumulates line-unit after line-unit to reach a sum (rather than a power) representing sheer mass enough to balance the momentum of the more quickly moving image-built portion (102-116) which completes the first verse paragraph of section III.

"Here" (93) is most nearly localized by "In a dim light" (95). The colon after "light" indicates the only degree of subordination the passage admits, and throws into prominence the "light," the series of whose (negative) characteristics constitutes the bulk of the sentence. Any intricacy here is of verbal interplay and rhetorical pattern, for the syntax is consciously simple. The "dim light" is "neither daylight . . . Nor darkness." "Daylight" is qualified by

    96 participial phrase plus prepositional phrase
    97 participial phrase plus prepositional phrase
    98 prepositional phrase plus participial phrase.

The second halves of 96 and 97 resemble "ablatives of specification" and modify their respective participles. 98 begins with an "ablative of means" which fits in two ways: it can modify "suggesting" maintaining the relation of the halves of the two lines preceding, with the latter of which it forms the figure of chiasmus; it can vary more than the word order if it modifies "Turning" in the line above and drops "suggesting" to the level of modifying "rotation." The word pattern increases the complexity:

```
97 Turning      transient
98 rotation     permanence
```

Each of the four structural units common to the three "day-light" lines (96-98) acts in turn as a kind of pylon to carry the new tensions created by their spatial conformation and semantic parallelism-and-antithesis. Nor has the order of their appearance in this figure

participle	adjective modifying object
	of preposition
object of preposition	object of participle

the logic of the grammatical sequence in either 96-97 or 98. Taking 96-97 as standard we read: 1) participle, 2) object of participle, 3) adjective modifying object of preposition, 4) object of preposition. Using the numbers only we can designate the figure under discussion as

```
1    3
4    2
```

The same lines (97-98) also present an alliterative pattern

```
Turning          transient
slow             suggesting
```

or

```
1    3
3    1
```

Once begun, the search for permutations reveals more:

```
96 form (forma)      lucid
97 shadow            beauty
```

or

```
2    3
2    4
```

Denoting the positions in the figure as

```
a    b
c    d
```

and using the symbol for congruence ∼, we can express the meaning-relationship of the terms in the two semantic figures as

$$96\text{-}97 \qquad a \sim d, \qquad b \not\sim c$$
$$97\text{-}98 \qquad a \sim c, \qquad b \not\sim c$$

Lines 99-101 deal with the functions of "darkness," also expressed in verbals. An infinitive of purpose is packed into the first line of the three ("Nor darkness to purify the soul") with its object and no modifiers to relieve its starkness or even to fill it out to the four usual stresses (we can of course read "Nor" with increased weight; the effect of compression is the same). The two participial lines alter the "daylight" pattern by omitting the adjectives in the prepositional phrase and offer a slight variation in the introduction of the definite article in the first (the participial) half of 100 and the second (the prepositional) half of 101.

Individual words throughout the passage reward scrutiny. There is nothing early-Yeatsian in this "dim" (95), which expresses neutrality rather than vagueness or mistiness. Yet the latter penumbra persists, as is the case with "Time before and time after" (94) regarded as yoked contradictories. The "dim light"-"daylight" chime is muffled; we tend to prolong "dim" because of the immediately adjacent second stress; only the caesural pause intervenes before the next stress, the first syllable of "neither,"[30] while "daylight" is attracted into the trochaic pattern which "neither's" very weak second syllable has set up.

The quiet dignity of 96 ("Investing form with lucid stillness")—it would be a perfect iambic pentameter line but for the suppression of the final stressed syllable—resides in the quality of the diction, arresting but not conspicuous. The pace is set by the solemn "Investing"—"clothing," or even "robing," in its place would produce a totally different effect. So "form," singular and thereby generalized, lifts us above a vaguely generic "forms" tied down to objects too indefinite to be individually (or even specifically) named. Form is invested, through the agency of light, with "stillness," which, although it denotes the absence of sound or motion (the presumption is in favor of the latter because of the recent association of the "still point" and the "turning world"), is presented as a positive quality. The stillness is characterized by lucidity, an attribute properly bestowed by light (when "lucid" means "resplendent" or, in astronomical terminology, "visible to the naked eye"), or otherwise dependent upon its presence (when "lucid" means "translucent"), or resembling it (when "lucid" figuratively describes what is clear to the mind). In the preceding section "a grace of sense" was spoken of as "a white light still and moving" (75). Daylight is white light par excellence and the norm for its composition of light of all wave lengths whose just proportions determine the (relatively) true perception of color. Although color words as such are rare in the *Quartets*, the analogy of truth to form (with daylight as standard of reference) would seem to hold. The stillness as *stasis* relates to the "ecstasy" (79) of the glimpsed "new world" (77). The connection is strengthened by the geographical connotation of "rotation" (98) and the veiled intransitive meaning of "turning" (97) which combine to allow a reading of "daylight" as synecdoche for "the turning world," whose motion (and the "white light" was "still" *and* "moving") emphasizes and coexists with the motionlessness of its exact center. The express manner in which daylight may be said to invest form with stillness we perhaps need not pursue exhaustively. It can be granted that form is already possessed of stillness which the daylight merely renders lucid. (It must not be forgotten that this and the following lines describe what is denied to the dim light of actuality. "Form" may also take on a meaning opposed to "matter.")

"Turning shadow into transient beauty" (97) momentarily reverses the rhythm. We are ordinarily not too conscious of "rising" or "falling" rhythms because of the indeterminate number of unaccented syllables (none or one or two or three) between stresses, but 96 and 97 form a contrasting pair of even-footed lines. The greater regularity of 97 accords with its greater ease of meaning, the cyclic sequence of day and night seen as light and shadow, or the lesser shadow only possible with sunlight cast in silhouette and tracery of ephemeral loveliness.

In 98 ("With slow rotation suggesting permanence") we return to deliberate iambics varied only by an extra slack syllable which accounts for the almost onomatopoeic effect of "rotation" in this line. "Rotation" as means or agent "suggesting permanence" does so by indirection. The inevitability of recurrence, inexorability perhaps (apt with "slow" as epithet), the circular path naturally symbolic of eternity, these lend to periodicity a semblance of permanence as opposed to flux.

The purifying darkness of line 99 and its affinities with that of St. John of the Cross have been given due attention in many quarters.[31] "Emptying" and "Cleansing" (100, 101), it is wholly purgative, but limited in its effects to the sensual and the affective. The higher powers of the soul are here untouched. The single means is "deprivation"; that from which affection is cleansed is "the temporal." The extension of the latter term in particular would be difficult to determine. Instead of building a body of doctrine or heresy on what Eliot leaves unsaid it would be safer to examine these lines in the light of their companion lines 96-98. The contrast is between the positive effects of daylight and the negative work of darkness. If "form" and "shadow" (96 and 97) are identified with unreality rather than immateriality the situation grows uncomfortably Platonic. Daylight would be something of a deceiver. (In section I "the pool was filled with water out of sunlight" [37].) Dim cave and bright day reverse roles. Darkness hollows out ("Emptying") where daylight cloaks over ("Investing"). Darkness operates on the unquestionably tangible "sensual"; daylight deals with elusive "form." Without going so far as to see illusion and annihilation as the only alternatives, we can accord to darkness the power of annihilating illusions ("a cloud passed, and the pool was empty" [41]). Darkness as it were dispels light instead of the reverse. A slight shift of emphasis makes light a creative force, darkness a destructive. But all these possibilities represent merely the underlying tensions which need in no way weaken Eliot's fundamentally Christian recognition of natural good vitiated by the Fall and by purgation made better. When we are eventually redeemed (the word occurs without the negating prefix only in *Little Gidding*, lines 208 and 236) it will still be "from time" ("All time is unredeemable" [BN 5]), but for the sake of "the timeless."

"Neither plenitude nor vacancy" (102) is an important transition half-line, offering one-word summations of the net contributions of daylight ("plenitude,") and darkness ("vacancy") in which three syllables recall three lines and much more besides. (Again we remember the pool of section I, "filled" [37] and "empty" [41].) Its extreme economy is further impressed upon us by the full stop which separates it from the passage descriptive of the denizens of the dim—and flickering—light. The choice of covering words is as always richly suggestive: "plenitude," of the fullness of creative possibility peopling all grades of the Great Chain of Being ("the enchainment of past and future" in line 81 can be thought of as referring to the gamut of temporal experience); "vacancy," of the attitude of expectancy we are bidden assume in the "Vacate et videte" of Psalm 45.

The "place of disaffection" becomes concrete in 102 ff. where the subway imagery[32] is strong enough to charge the second and briefer reference, *East Coker* 119-122, with its peculiar power.

```
102                    Only a flicker
103  Over the strained time-ridden faces
104  Distracted from distraction by distraction
105  Filled with fancies and empty of meaning
106  Tumid apathy with no concentration
107  Men and bits of paper, whirled by the cold wind
108  That blows before and after time,
109  Wind in and out of unwholesome lungs
110  Time before and time after.
111  Eructation of unhealthy souls
112  Into the faded air, the torpid
113  Driven on the wind that sweeps the gloomy
       Hills of London,
114  Hampstead and Clerkenwell, Campden and Putney,
115  Highgate, Primrose and Ludgate. Not here
116  Not here the darkness, in this twittering world.
```

Although the fourteen and a half lines contain no finite verb there is a syntax of rhetoric which builds meaningfully with its spider web system of suspensions and relations. The first noun, "flicker" (102), is in form and function almost a verb, and is modified by the adverb-sounding "only" and "Over..." phrase. We unconsciously emend the opening to "[There is] only a flicker" or "[The dim light]...flicker[s]" and are free to devote our attention to the haunting faces"— how different from the "petals on a wet black bough" which

may be permitted to provide contrast and implicit commentary on two poetic approaches to human experience—
from which depend equally the next two lines (104 and 105)
and which start the (distinct) comparative reflections of 106
and 107. The last word of the latter line, "wind," begins a new
series with its clause-modifier, 108, and appositive, 109, and,
after the strangely interpolated refrain, 110 (which ends with a
period), its resumption into "Eructation" and development
through the incantatory place names which as wind's course
(not tube stops—they are common to no transit route) have
more than an alliterative significance. Plotted on a sectional map
of London these seven "hills" (is there irony in the number?)
describe a closed curve resembling a spiral turned in upon itself
(instead of extended into infinity):

	(5) Highgate
(1) Hampstead	(6) Primrose
	(2) Clerkenwell
	(7) Ludgate
(4) Putney	
	(3) Campden

Even the sequence of their initials bears out the reiterated
imagery[33] of greater and smaller eddies of "turning world"
(section II), "rotation" (98), "whirled" (107):

L[ondon, the whole]

H   C   C   P
H   P   L

The entire passage 102-116 is curiously compelling, full of
unexpected ramifications and returns. Its rhythmic shifts tantal-
ize. "Only a flicker/Over the strained time-ridden faces" (102-
103) is sufficiently dactyllic to create the illusion of a hexameter
line; this it is that lengthens "strained," whose temporal equivalence to "time-ridden" suggests their synonymity, or at least the
taken-for-grantedness of the latter term as accounting for the
condition "strained" denotes.

"Distracted from distraction by distraction" (104) with three
identical main stresses in predominantly iambic movement at-
tracts secondary stresses to both intermediate prepositions by
the very fact of the word play.

"Filled with fancies and empty of meaning" (105) reverts to the characteristic four-stress pattern, heard the more strongly for the alliterated "f's" of the first half-line and the subdued but perceptible "m's" of the second. The metrical symmetry is marked: "Filled with"// "meaning," "fancies and" // "empty of." The sense echo of the plenitude-vacancy summary of 102 can be construed as conveying an almost bitter irony, as does the pairing in 107 of "Men and bits of paper," equally the wind's sport.

"Tumid apathy" (106) stands in much the same relation to the line before as "Neither plenitude nor vacancy" (102) to the six lines it follows: emptiness is manifested by "apathy" to which experience is meaningless, "Filled" becomes "Tumid," and the travesty is complete. "With no concentration" (106) relates to "Distracted" above (104) and "whirled" below (107) and indicates once more the difference between this neuter, unfocussed existence and awareness at the vital and constant center, the "still point," which gives gravitational coherence to the variable surface of the "turning world." Disorder arises from "distraction," pulling away— and this in conflicting directions ("Distracted from distraction by distraction" [104])—and from the further errancy of whirling resistless and with no fixed center.

The general debility of the disaffected is borne out by the physical diction: "Tumid apathy" (106), "unwholesome lungs" (109), "Eructation," "unhealthy" (111), "faded," "torpid" (112). This class of half-alives has been a concern of Eliot's even from Prufrock days—the dwellers in the thousand furnished rooms, the damp-souled housemaids, the Laodiceans attacked in *The Hippopotamus*, the ante-hell population of *The Waste Land, The Hollow Men*. Many phrases in 102ff. recall the earlier people who were neither hot nor cold, and in this inconsequentially "twittering world" (116) not even the cold "wind that sweeps" (113) is genuinely sanative; we and they need the fire of *Little Gidding*, to which the darkness sought here and not found is paradoxical prelude.

The "cold wind" (107) seems originally to have been outside of time, blowing "before and after time" (108), but it too is drawn into the vortex as "Wind in and out of unwholesome lungs" (109) in "Time before and time after" (110) which as line 94 provided a temporal setting for

observations made in the "place of disaffection." The classical
association of wind and spirit shares the prevalent degradation in "Eructation of unhealthy souls" (111). The atmosphere of stagnation is intensified by "air" in 112 as opposed
to "wind" elsewhere, and its epithet "faded," besides having
the force of the French *fade*, affects by transference the
characteristic colorlessness of perception in the "dim light."
"Torpid" (112) and therefore "Driven" (113) presumably
modify "souls" (111) whose plight echoes in Dantesque
fashion the lot of the unburied in *Aeneid* VI denied access to
the farther shore, likened to leaves[34] in autumn in their fitful
flight and to migrant birds surprised by winter. Is this image
behind "twittering" in the last line of tha passage? There are,
too, those other dead who "did squeak and gibber in the
Roman streets." But this (pagan) darkness is not that which
purifies. We must

117   Descend lower, descend only
118   Into the world of perpetual solitude,
119   World not world, but that which is not world,
120   Internal darkness, deprivation
121   And destitution of all property,
122   Dessication of the world of sense,
123   Evacuation of the world of fancy,
124   Inoperancy of the world of spirit;
125   This is the one way, and the other
126   Is the same, not in movement
127   But abstention from movement; while the world
       moves
128   In appetency, on its metalled ways
129   Of time past and time future.

The second verse paragraph of section III opens with a
pair of Eliot's rare imperatives. Our descent is to be lower—
and harder—than that into Avernus. The tone of 117 is
prophetic, its rhythm sonorous:

Dĕscēnd lōwĕr,⁄⁄ dĕscēnd ōnlў

The next few lines exhibit the verbal prestidigitation of
Donne and Andrewes and the sentiments of St. John of the
Cross. We deal with successive "worlds" (122-124) as
differing areas of experience, with the one enduring "world"

(118 and the first word of 119) as the liberating element, and with "world" (119) in its Gospel connotation of hostility to the things of the spirit. The caution to "descend only / Into the world of perpetual solitude" (117-118) is at first puzzling; it appears to make an end of a mere means—"perpetual solitude" would be a poor substitute for perpetual light—but with *Little Gidding* as a corrective we can read the emphasis here on the necessary aloneness of the soul before God rather than on union with God with which Eliot at this point is not explicitly concerned.

The descent is into several states beginning with "d" and abounding in consonants. The sound pattern moves easily into the phrasal pattern of the identically constructed 122-124. The Latin roots are close to the surface and the economy of diction all the more striking for "of the world of" charm-like thrice repeated. The "internal darkness" is not without conflict: *privare* can mean "bereave" or "deliver," *destituere*, "abandon" or "defraud" or "fasten down." "Property" (121) seems as much "selfhood" or "essential characteristic" as "possession." The unselving is to be carried on on the three levels of "sense" (122), "fancy" (123) and "spirit" (124). On the first ("Desiccation of the world of sense") *siccare* gives us the meanings "dry," "drain," "empty" met in the garden context of section I which we equate with the "world of sense." On the second ("Evacuation of the world of fancy") we have a specific antidote to the condition of line 105 ("Filled with fancies"). The third level ("Inoperancy of the world of spirit") is more subtle as the realm of "inner freedom from the practical desire" (72) not to be confused with the "apathy" of line 106 and a possible Quietist construction. Behind "inoperancy" is *operari* with its multiple meaning—"work," "have effect," "serve," "weave," "perform rites." This suspension of faculties is "the one way" (125), the way down of the epigraph, and the other that is the same would be the way up of intuitive perception at the still point, "not in movement / But abstention from movement." Meanwhile the (opposing) world counters "abstention" with "appetency," stillness with movement (on the rigidly predetermined and time-bound "metalled ways" of the underground railroad with its unresisting human freight), timelessness with "time past and time future" unresolved into eternal presence.

The brief lyric that is section IV surpasses everything else in Eliot for sheer music and a dance-like quality resident in the free rhythms and differing line lengths. Without questioning whether he has yielded to the fascination of the sound play, delicate, nowhere excessive, we are sure that here is poetry which communicates before it is understood.

130 Time and the bell have buried the day,
131 The black cloud carries the sun away.
132 Will the sunflower turn to us, will the clematis
133 Stray down, bend to us; tendril and spray
134 Clutch and cling?
135 Chill
136 Fingers of yew be curled
137 Down on us? After the kingfisher's wing
138 Has answered light to light, and is silent, the
                                              light is still
139 At the still point of the turning world.

Lightness and sway derive from the placing of the stresses, the many natural dactyls ("sunflower," "clematis," "king-fisher's") and phrases readily so scanned ("turn to us," "bend to us," "Down on us")—in these examples and in "Time and the," "tendril and," "Fingers of," the stressed syllable is closed by a nasal—tha alliteration in "cl" and the prevalence of "l" (it occurs in every line but 137), the internal rhyme and echo generally.

The opening couplet is a signally successful example of imagery-by-means-of-rhythm. The weighted "Time" and the voiced initial consonants are spaced quite literally to toll the knell of parting day, and to this effect the "extra" slack syllables, the definite article before "bell" and "day," contribute not a little. The enforced slowness of enunciating "black cloud" brings the dead march to its eventual period. But at the same time we are beguiled into seeing "hurries" in a superimposed "buried-carries" and so anticipate the change of tempo the next line introduces. This (132) takes up "sun" in "sunflower" and the "cl" of "cloud" in "clematis," to be continued in "clutch and cling" (134). "Day" and "away" are heard again in the interesting formation of 133:

Stray ... bend ... tendril ... spray

Similar correspondences are "Will" (twice in 132), the unstressed second syllable of "tendril," "Chill" (135) and "still" (138 and 139); "cling" (134), "Fingers" (136) and "Kingfisher's wing" (137). There are two groups of assonances: "cloud," "-flower," "down" (131-133) and the more distant "Down" of 137; "light," "light," "silent," "light" (all in 138) and the remote "Time" (130).

After the obsequies of 130 and 131, the poet seems more than ever concerned with our relations with the inanimate (but living) natural world. Are we, in eclipse, lords of creation still? He is not sure of Clytie's deference, but there is wistful tenderness ("tender" and "lingering" are seldom at home in contemporary poetic idiom, but they can be read by a Joycean verbal legerdemain in "tendril" and the "cling" group) in the graceful clematis (one is hard put to it not to point out "beauties" in this exquisite interlude), while the thought of our own passing (or immortality?) comes with the "Chill/Fingers" (135-136) of funereal yew.

The flashing iridescence of the plumage of the bird in flight literally answers "light to light" (138) and its subsequent silence is not strictly synaesthetic.[35] If the kingfisher be identified with the halcyon of ancient legend there is a new wealth of grief allayed and peaceful brooding "At the still point of the turning world" (139).

Section V, like the corresponding sections of *East Coker* and *Little Gidding*, is (in part) directly concerned with the artist-craftsman's problem of the limitations of his medium. In his words about words Eliot displays the maximum control and inevitable frustration of the master of an elusive art form and the knower of things unsayable.

    140 Words move, music moves
    141 Only in time; but that which is only living
    142 Can only die. Words, after speech, reach
    143 Into the silence. Only by the form, the pattern,
    144 Can words or music reach
    145 The stillness, as a Chinese jar still
    146 Moves perpetually in its stillness.
    147 Not the stillness of the violin, while the note
         lasts,
    148 Not that only, but the co-existence,

149 Or say that the end precedes the beginning,
150 And the end and beginning were always there
151 Before the beginning and after the end.
152 And all is always now. . . .

As at other turning points, our attention is called to new
matter for emphasis, or to old matter for new emphasis, by a
terse four-word line (elsewhere a medial "and" may make a
fifth) in which each word contains a strongly accented
syllable and often no other, and in which one of the words is
used twice, once in each half-line, with rather solemn effect.
So "Time present and time past" (1), "Time past and time
future" (46 and 85), "Time before and time after" (94 and
110), "Descend lower, descend only" (117), and, here, "Words
move, music moves."

To the analogies traceable in the conduct of words and
music— not random words but words in order, as music is
ordered sound distinguished from "noise" by the regularity
of vibration of the body which produces it and which
therefore in another sense "moves only in time"—Eliot has
given mature and un-Lanier like consideration in his *Music of
Poetry*.

The relation of pattern to background, words or music to
silence, movement to stillness, succession to presence,
occupies 141-152 middle. (These lines should be reread in the
light of 162-172—"The detail of the pattern is movement,
[etc.]"—near the end of *Burnt Norton*.) Tenuous, terminable
("that which is only living/Can only die." [141-142]), this
relation approaches absorption as its limit ("Words , after
speech, reach/Into the silence." [142-143]). Four "only's" (all
adverbs) in three lines represent the effort to be explicit, to
clear away the irrelevant. The use of explanatory appositive
("the form, the pattern" [143]), simile (the Chinese jar of
145), repetition ("moves," "stillness"), correction and
alternate ("Not that only, but . . ." [148], "Or say that
. . . [149]) indicates the difficulty of the effort. Another
feature making for tension is the opposition between line
units (to which we have grown so accustomed as to accept
line-ends as adequate punctuation) and thought units: lines
140-146 consist of three sentences beginning or ending (or
both) mid-line. Their respective subjects, interestingly

enough, are "Words"-"music," "Words," "words or music;"
the predicate verbs are "move(s)," "reach," "can reach." The
two clauses neglected in the above schematization articulate
significantly with the noticed clauses of sentences one and
three and with each other. Thus the living complex of 141
either contrasts with the deliberately simplified "Words...
music" or in some way embraces them in its fated death; the
"Chinese jar" is the model of attainment of the desired end of
"words or music." Further, the living (and presumbaly
animate) ends in death (cessation of movement), the
inanimate "Moves perpetually." The materially organic
disintegrates, the formally organized perdures. The second
sentence (142-143) reveals that "Words" belong to both
realms. "After speech," i.e., living and temporal use
("mov[ing] in time"), they aspire to the condition of silence,
which here seems to imply infinity rather than negation. The
combined "speech, reach" (142) are especially prominent
against the background of short "i's:"

```
140                    -ic
141  in      which is      living
142                    (speech, reach)
143  In-
144                             (reach)
145    still-          still
146          in its  stillness
```

The "ly" ending occurring four times in "only" and once
more in "perpetually" seems because of its lack of stress (and
its shorter and lax pronunciation, particularly before a
consonant in English speech) to be closer to the true short "i"
that the full [i:] sound (and "Chinese" is not very much
stronger[36]). The weak vowels in "after," "the" (four times),
"silence," "pattern," "stillness" (twice), "a," "perpetually," "but"
(in this context), the not very long "u" in "music" (twice) and
"perpetually" shading into "move(s)" (three times), the similar
"o" series in the "only's" and "form"-"or" and, modified, in
"words," give a gradation as of grays and olive scarcely
relieved by the splashes of flat "a"—"that," "can," "after,"[37]
"pattern," "can," "as"—only one of which is in a stressed
position. There is, though, a striking recurrence of the single
rich vowel in "time," "die" "silence" (141-143), each the first

important word in its line and coming before a decided pause. These, and the negligible "by" (143), prepare us for the brilliance, vocalic and symbolic, of the delayed image, "Chinese jar" (145), which, whatever be the ulterior values,[38] exemplifies the perfection of its class of artifact and the embodiment of a naturally contemplative spirit. The unobtrusive play on "still" (adverb) and "stillness" points up the latent ambiguity of "perpetually" (146)—is it within or outside of time?—and the paradox of "Moves...in...stillness." The stillness we have met before, but always as a point having intensity rather than duration. In section I it was the presences that "moved...in a formal pattern" (32). Here it is "words or music" that by moving thus reach their term of realization. In addition, the double meaning of "still" alerts us to the hinted transitive function of "moves" (146) as predicate of "Chinese jar"—the latter certainly evokes aesthetic response, as will "words or music" if so ordered as to "reach/The stillness" that is the percipient's.

The sound image in 147 is a further development of the notion of "stillness." The strange "sentence" it begins at first rejects ("Not the stillness of the violin"), then partially readmits ("Not that only") the new comparison. The meaning of "motionlessness" is closer than ever to that of "silence" even in the implicit contradiction between line-halves. As long as "the note lasts" the "stillness" of the instrument is but apparent—both string and resonating box are in vibration. This is, in a practical sense, the "co-existence" (148) of sound and stillness, sound *in* stillness, pattern against background. (And the violin as the closest instrumental approximation to the human voice is a fitting equivalent for "words or music.") "Co-existence" is also to be explained by the conclusion that "all is always now" (152) after the three end-and-beginning lines (149-151) which anticipate the refrain of *East Coker* in their variations on the time theme that has pervaded *Burnt Norton*. We are nearer affirmation here than at the tentative opening of the first *Quartet*. "End" may parallel "time future," "beginning" "time past," but both are seen *sub specie aeternitatis* in an unconditional "always now" beside the "If...eternally present" of line 4. "The end precedes the beginning" at the nodes of the bowed string rich in overtones, in the Chinese dragon, tail in mouth, in the intuitive knowledge words are found for in the formal pattern, an objective correlative of deeper than emotional significance. "And the end and the beginning were always there" in the inchoate speech of the poet whose pattern yet eludes him, in the divine foreknowledge and creative will Eliot sees reflected faintly in the poet's making. (A few lines farther we have specific reference to the Incarnate Word of God "in the desert" [158], the arena of the human spirit at strife with the spirit of "this twittering world.") "Before the beginning and after the end" as much amplifies "there" in the preceding line as it supplies an impalpable "then" for events or conditions in this continuum of experience which both transcends ordinary space-time and exceeds the ordinary power of expression of human words.

152   Words strain,
153 Crack and sometimes break, under the burden,
154 Under the tension, slip, slide, perish,
155 Decay with imprecision, will not stay in place,
156 Will not stay still.

Nine verbs in three lines and two halves largely dispensing with connectives convey the poet's exasperation with his intractable or oversoft materials, whose ineptitude has causes both intrinsic, their native "imprecision" (155), and extrinsic, "the burden," "the tension" (153-154) of the utterance they are whipped into rising to. The bi-dimensional pressure, vertical-downward ("burden") and horizontal-outward ("tension"), exposes the flaws of rational communication faced with what is above and beyond its fallen nature. The disabilities are paired, the pairs interwoven: "Words strain" (152) "Under the tension" (154), "Crack...break, under the burden" (153); "slip" (154)-"will not stay in place" (155), "slide" (154)-"Will not stay still" (156), "perish (154)-"Decay" (155). The phrasal and alliterative pairings now support, now interfere (but the interference only reveals other likenesses): "break"-"burden," "under the burden"-"Under the tension," "slip"-"slide," "will not stay in place"-"Will not stay still." Assonance and internal rhyme occur at fairly close range: "Words"-"burden," "Crack"-"break," "Decay"-"stay," "Will"-"still." A triplet pattern links the last two groups:

Decay	will	stay
Will	stay	still

Predominantly monosyllabic, these lines give a somewhat high word-count and a distinct sense of crowding, as if numbers could repair the insufficiency of breadth and firmness.

By an almost imperceptible transition the mechanical "Words" that crack and break shade into something closer to the living "voices" of 156. "Decay" and "perish" are properly used of organic substances, "will not stay," suggests volition as well as futurity. The relation set up in the next sentence is vividly imaged:

156   Shrieking voices
157 Scolding, mocking, or merely chattering,
158 Always assail them.

"Them" can refer only to the "Words" already disparaged and now seen beset as it were by demons whose present participial activity represents the degradation to which nobler-purposed words are subject. As usual there is an interesting relationship among initial letters—"*Sh*rieking," "*Sc*olding," "*ch*attering." "Mocking" and "merely" alliterate simply. "Always assail" illustrates syllabic gymnastics not too often indulged in: the stressed elements "al-" and "-sail" have a common letter-sequence, a-l, as do the unstressed "-ways" and "as-," a-s; the first syllables of the two words are similarly constructed, "al-," "as-," but do not sound alike, while the second syllables, "-ways," "-sail," rhyme in reverse.

The audacious comparison which follows is actually a revelation of Eliot's profound respect for the word as redemptive agent in that other desert, the "place of disaffection" with its mocking and chattering fancies and distractions.

158   The Word in the desert
159 Is most attacked by voices of temptation,
160 The crying shadow in the funeral dance,
161 The loud lament of the disconsolate chimera.

The exact application of "most" (159) gives us pause. Is it in comparison with the words of discourse that the Word of God is "most attacked," or are "voices of temptation" being compared in His regard with the scolding, mocking, merely chattering voices just above? In either event it is the "voices of temptation" that lead into the next two lines which stand to them (the voices) in a kind of apposition that is explained by the original term before it can illuminate it. Included, then, in the "voices" are the "crying shadow" of 160 and the "loud lament" of 161, while the structural parallels lead us to relate to "temptation" the "funeral dance" and the "disconsolate chimera." This need not be an oversimplification if the relation is kept open and not restricted to absolute equation. The two lines in question are also strongly linked with each other: "shadow" with "chimera" by the note of illusoriness in both their meanings, "dance" with "lament" as complementary physical—and formal—expressions of grief, "crying" with "loud" insofar as both indicate audibility, "crying" with "disconsolate" as effect-and-cause, "funeral" with "lament" as cause-and-effect, "crying" with "chimera" and "dance" with "disconsolate" by alliteration, and finally whole line with whole line by similarity of structure: "the"—adjective-noun-preposition-"the"—adjective-noun.

It would be helpful to know what particular feature of primitive ritual Eliot had in mind for the "crying shadow" in his "funeral dance"—cheated devil, unpropitiated deity, official mourner, uneasy spirit of the departed (the closeness of "shadow" to "shade" favors this)? There would be rhetorical justification for identifying the "crying shadow" once and for all with the "disconsolate chimera;" "loud lament" could in this case be read as in apposition with "funeral dance:"

> The crying shadow   in the funeral dance
> The loud lament   of the disconsolate chimera

The chimera as composite of lion, goat and serpent is an apt representative of the adversary who goes about seeking whom he may devour, of the chief of the damned on the left hand segregated from the sheep, and of the tempter who chose the serpent's guise in Eden; the "disconsolate chimera" can well be Satan discomfited. The father of lies and master of illusion is fittingly masked as a figment of the diseased imagination, and to complete the involvement, the "funeral dance" can be thought of as signalling the end of his undisputed sway.

The last seventeen lines of *Burnt Norton* distill the essence
of the one hundred sixty-one before them, and add a positive
note not hitherto made explicit. Line 166 contains the first
mention of love as supreme motive power; 163 is perhaps the
most comprehensively allusive line in all of eliot, embracing
as it does the content of chapters 19 and 20 of book II of the
Dark Night of the Soul. The passage opens:

> 162   The detail of the pattern is movement,
> 163 As in the figure of the ten stairs.

The pattern has been claimed (143-145) as the means by
which words reach the stillness. Its detail is here recognized
as movement, *as*—we are dealing with analogy not identity—
St. John of the Cross pictures the outset of the soul's search
for God via the mystic ladder, a search which is ultimately to
lead to infused contemplation. This and its aesthetic
counterpart are not rigorously distinguished, to the vast
enrichment of the latter.

Having set the stage by this categorical statement ending
with an almost self-conscious period, the poet goes on to
select a main difference between desire and love and to
develop this through a series of modifying lines whose
precise application presents some slight ambiguities.

> 164 Desire itself is movement
> 165 Not in itself desirable;
> 166 Love is itself unmoving,
> 167 Only the cause and end of movement,
> 168 Timeless, and undesiring
> 169 Except in the aspect of time
> 170 Caught in the form of limitation
> 171 Between un-being and being.

We are very conscious of pattern in the repetitions,
modulations and placing of words. "Itself" is pivotal in 164-
166; the syllabic arrangement of the three lines is very
similar: the endings of the first and third, "is movement,"
"unmoving," correspond closely in meter and vowel value; so
do the beginnings of the second and third, "Not in," "Love
is." The only variants are themselves intimately related,
"Desire" with its postponed stress on the seeming syllable-

-and-a-half, and "desirable" with the extra slack which emphasizes the pause the punctuation urges.

The rhythmic shift to a three-beat unit suggests comparison with 64-71 in section II where, however, two such units form each long line. Eight of these are a near equivalent of the seventeen short lines of the conclusion. Both deal with time and movement, but for the "still point" of the earlier section we now recognize "Love" as focus and perhaps radiant center.

167 ends with the third occurrence within six lines of "movement" in this position: "detail...is movement" (162), "Desire...is movement" (164), but "Love is.../Only the cause and end of movement" (167). The "pattern" is in a sense the "end" of its detail. By legitimate substitution of similarly equated terms we deduce that the pattern (the means to stillness) *is* love (the end, stillness itself). According to the epigraph, the way up and the way down are the same; here the means and end seem to be one, the way is truly unitive. We remember that the Word said, "I am the Way," and appreciate the suggestion in 166-167 of Prime Mover and Uncaused Cause.

"Timeless, and undesiring" (168) are best interpreted as modifying "Love," with whose first predicate adjective, "unmoving," their formation tallies. The comma after "Timeless" inclines us to read over the line-end, grouping "undesiring/Except in the aspect of time." "Caught, [etc.]" (170-171) will then also modify "Love" and explain the apparent contradiction of love's averred absence of desire by the exigencies of its assumed "form [not the "form" of 143 which was synonymous with "pattern"] of limitation." The implications are increasingly Incarnational. "Between un-being and being" imposes a strange limitation indeed. (And the diction increases the strangeness—the triple "be-" calls attention to the more obscure vowel-plus-nasal element which accompanies each occurrence, as "*un*-being," "a*nd* being" and, backwards, "bet*ween*," where the reversal gives to the second syllable the additional function of approximating by its length and force the disyllabic "being.") Instead of trying to insert a middle term between the contradictories "un-being" and "being" we might regard them as two ways of describing the same phenomenon, the *exinanivit semetipsum* which is both an abrogating and a becoming; in another sense it is true that any creature is "between being and unbeing."

172 ff., though separately punctuated and recalling the final image of section I, rather burst out of the foregoing with the relief of concrete realization.

> 172 Sudden in a shaft of sunlight
> 173 Even while the dust moves
> 174 There rises the hidden laughter
> 175 Of children in the foliage
> 176 Quick now, here, now, always—
> 177 Ridiculous the waste sad time
> 178 Stretching before and after.

There are "s's" in 172 in the "b" positions of 171. The two "su's" are picked up by "us" in "dust" below and between them. 172 and 174 offer the half-rhymes "sudden" and "hidden" as well as the truer "shaft" and "laughter." Other sound links are found in "sun*l*ight," "wh*i*le" and "*ri*ses" in the same three lines which complement the earlier group, "T*im*eless," "undes*ir*ing," "*tim*e" (168-169) (it will be observed that the two sets of three also represent three combinations of two letters each, im-ir-im-li-il-ri). "Even" in 173 links the weak syllables of "sudden" and "hidden" and repeats the dominant vowel of 171. "Moves" at the end of 173 reemphasizes its cognates in 162, 164, 166 and 167 and with its subject, "dust," brings out anew the positive note we are sensible of in this conclusion—we remember "dust" only in its passive role as object of "Disturbing" in line 17. Similarly "laughter" in 174 is subject of "rises" while in 43 it was object of "containing." 174-175 constitute a delicately and pleasingly varied rephrasing of 42-43. The "perpetual slight novelty" of the whole passage renders it more effective as reminiscence (which though reminiscence of a *memory* seems to have the algebraic effect of a double negative in reviving the actual experience) than repetition could be. Further, the intervening sections have drawn the soul in the way of darkness, which the "shaft of sunlight" now dispels with a kind of Paschal brightness, freeing the purified vision for the more immediate apprehension of "our first world" (23 and 24)

restored, where the laughing children and the bird cry
(" ... here, now, always" [176]) are conjured up in the dancing
motes "out of heart of light" (39), and sound and light are
fused in the intensely realized present which nullifies the
"waste sad time / Stretching before and after." This non-
present has become "ridiculous," unworthy of serious
consideration, but there is more pathos than contempt in the
slow and labored syllables which follow the rapid four of the
initial and dismissing adjective, "Ridiculous," which echoes
the impatience of "Quick" above.

ℱ 2 ℱ

East Coker

EAST COKER is of all the *Quartets* the most heavily commented upon as to philosophical content and bearing.[1] The present study makes no attempt to add anything to this line of discussion, but merely offers some findings with regard to the disposition and correlation of the most elementary structural units.

The opening phrase, "In my beginning is my end," fills substantially the same role as *Burnt Norton's* "Time present and time past," recurring as motif, whole line or fragment, in duplicate or variation, until the closing half-line which restores the order of the original motto of Mary Queen of Scots, "In my end is my beginning." Throughout, tonal echoes of *Burnt Norton* establish a perceptible if subtle bond between the first two *Quartets* even where the rhythmic patterns differ conspicuously. Thus in the modified blank verse (basically six-stress, but tending rather to weaken one or more of the stresses than to break in the middle) of *East Coker's* first section we find speculation on the work of time followed by the concretely imaged "you" passage with its strange light, shimmering heat and elusive vision ("If you do not come too close") or perhaps locution—sound is possibly a stronger feature in *East Coker* than in *Burnt Norton*. (Incidentally, the "echoes" here are historical rather than personal.)

The longer lines which are characteristic of *East Coker* in general and the heavier blocks in which they are paragraphed make for greater solemnity and seeming regularity. This and a more formal rhetoric are especially apparent in the first section, which we come to after the abbreviated and allusive coda of *Burnt Norton*.

1 In my beginning is my end. In succession
2 Houses rise and fall, crumble, are extended,
3 Are removed, destroyed, restored, or in their place
4 Is an open field, or a factory, or a by-pass.
5 Old stone to new building, old timber to new fires,
6 Old fires to ashes, and ashes to the earth
7 Which is already flesh, fur and faeces,
8 Bone of man and beast, cornstalk and leaf.
9 Houses live and die: there is a time for building
10 And a time for living and for generation
11 And a time for the wind to break the loosened pane
12 And to shake the wainscot where the field-mouse trots
13 And to shake the tattered arras woven with a silent motto

Asyndeton (2-3) and anaphora (5-6, 10-13), alliteration (7, notably) and assonance (passim), climax (or descent—5-6 ["timber" to "earth"], 11-13) and antithesis (2, 5, 9), chiasmus (2) and ellipsis (in the verbless "main clause" of the third sentence [5-8]) are among the devices which enter into the shaping of the first of the three strophic units of section I.

The procession of predicates of the successive "Houses" (2) begins the confirmation by example of the initial thematic statement. Of the seven verbs three represent beginnings of a sort—"rise," "are extended," "[are] restored"—while the remaining four—"fall," "crumble" "Are removed," "[are] destroyed" (2-3)—and the three suggested replacements— "open field," "factory," "by-pass" (4)—swing the balance to the end. This is consistent with the emphasis of the opening words, which saw the end in the beginning rather than the reverse. The order of the predicates may be expressed in these terms as: beginning-end-end-beginning / end-end-beginning / end-end-end.

The houses in question are actual material houses ("stone," "timber") and not families, although this figure can support a wealth of symbolism beneath its literal meaning. One wonders why the poet has employed quite so many verbs to express what are basically only two alternatives, but the effect produced by the multiplication is that of having foreseen and exhausted all contingencies, besides illustrating the problematical imprecision of words which the last section of *Burnt Norton* has deplored. Similarly the nouns are reducible to two extremes of indignity, disuse and common utility.

End-and-beginning likewise dominate 5-8, in the same proportion—"building" is constructive, "fires" and "ashes" can hardly be so regarded (except for the latent symbolism of "new fires" in connection with the purification motif and a potential Paschal connotation[2]). With 5 and 6 in particular we detect the accents of folk-charm observed in the corresponding part of *Burnt Norton*, although here too a certain sophistication creeps in with the absence of epithet for "ashes" and "earth," and a note of irony in the catalogue of decayed substances whose common end is earth.

Lettering and word rhythms throughout these lines reveal unexpected linkings. All the "f's" seem to belong to the "fall" category—"field," "factory," "fires," "flesh, fur and faeces," even "leaf" which inverts the prevailing f-l sequence. The vowel of "Old stone" (5) is approached gradually through the series "removed, destroyed, restored," maintained with relapses as far as "Bone" (8), and revived only in 13, "woven" and "motto." The nervous "or's" of 3 and 4 with their limited conjunctive force give way to the anvil line 5 whose heavy juxtaposed stresses can be read as eight beats. The uncertain fate of "Houses" is mirrored in the rhythmic contradictions. The falling rhythm of most of line 2 is sharply reversed in the next line where the auxiliary tends to be overlooked in the movement of "removed, destroyed, restored" to the final stressed "place." A second reversal in line 4 shakes more than it reestablishes our original sense of rhythmic direction.

Paired sounds occurring at irregular distances effect a strange reticulation that links each line with every other: "end" (1)-"extended" (2), "crumble" (2)-"timber" (5), "stone" (5)-"Bone" (8), "ashes" (6)-"flesh" (7), "break" (11) -"shake" (12,13), "Houses" (2,9)-"-mouse" (12), "pane" (11) - "wainscot" (12), "trots" (12)-"motto" (13). The same is true of word and phrase: "Houses" (2, 9), "are" as auxiliary (2, 3), "field" (4, 12), "Old" (5, 6), "fires" (5, 6), "building" (5, 9), "live" and "living" (9, 10), "a time for" (9, 10, 11), "And to shake the" (12, 13). Line to line alliteration is especially telling in 11-13—"wind," "wainscot where," "woven;" "-mouse," "motto." Repetitions within lines—"In" (1), "or" (4), "old" (5), "ashes" (6)—intensify the inbreeding.

The shape of the whole passage reminds us of a form not to be sought for in the Eliot repertoire. Lines 4 and 8 end with periods and together comprise an acceptable sonnet octave (with great metrical liberties, of course). Our "sestet" is crowded into five lines but its general thematic relation to the eight lines above satisfies content requirements. The utmost ingenuity can discover nothing Petrarchan about any substitute for a rhyme scheme, but with the hint of "trots"-"motto" (12-13) we can fancy not quatrains but more quasi-couplets: "place"-"-pass" (3-4) is least unconvincing; "succession"-"extended" (1-2) shows both an antepenult half-rhyme, "u[x]"-"ex," and the reversed rhyme, "[x]e"- "ex," which also relates *"faeces"* and *"leaf"* (7-8); "fires" and "earth" (5-6) cannot in English pronunciation claim even a common vowel-plus-r; "building," "generation" and "pane" (9, 10, 11) go alone, leaving the final "trots"-"motto" the added force of revived rhyme. 5 and 6, 10 and 11, 12 and 13 could also be coupled by initial identity, "Old," "And a time for," "And to shake the," respectively, and this is consistent with the end-grouping first attempted.

The groping quality of the diction of the first lines of the passage gives place towards the end to a series of cameos restrained and perfect in their evocative power. The transition comes with "Houses live and die" which parallels the "Houses rise and fall" of the second line and introduces a more human valuation than the impersonal cycles decribed above were susceptible of. This is generalized in 9 and 10, while 11-13, poignant and particular, image the decline with the master strokes of shaken "wainscot" and "tattered arras" where the two nouns aptly convey the character of the departed glory. Minute accuracy is further exemplified in the choice of "trots" to render the locomotion of the "field-mouse," so distinguished from the domestic variety which runs closer to the ground and as if on wheels. The "tattered arras" with its "silent motto" is the last vestige of defeated speech to survive the irrational shattering and rattling we have imagined hearing beneath the actual words of 11-13 ("shake," "tattered," "break the loosened pane") where no noise of such is specified.

In the next block of verses we choose one of the endings that awaited the "Houses" above, an "open field" for former mansion site.

14 In my beginning is my end. Now the light falls
15 Across the open field, leaving the deep lane
16 Shuttered with branches, dark in the afternoon,
17 Where you lean against a bank while a van passes,
18 And the deep lane insists on the direction
19 Into the village, in the electric heat
20 Hypnotised. In a warm haze the sultry light
21 Is absorbed, not refracted, by grey stone.
22 The dahlias sleep in the empty silence.
23 Wait for the early owl.

The time is afternoon, as in the garden of *Burnt Norton* and on the road to *Little Gidding*. (Is this time, like the "always four o'clock" of the Mad Tea Party, the least trammeled by reminders of its passage, and so closest to the "timeless?") "You" are not in the field but in the lane which the light has left. The late summer somnolence is over all. The rhythm is unhurried, the vocabulary quiet and largely monosyllabic— the ten lines from 14-23 contain only twenty-one polysyl- lables, three of them such solely by virtue of their inflectional endings—the syntax normal with no violence to word order or punctuation and a fair degree of unambiguous subordination. "L" and "n" are the most frequent individual consonants but their function is rather to bind together the rich and varied vowel fabric than to form a distinct pattern of their own. The simple iteration of "the deep lane" tacitly forwards the meaning of its verb in 18, "insists," one of the few arresting words in this peace-betokening context. "Hypnotised" is perhaps another, and is also predicated of the lane. It to some extent anticipates by its suggestiveness the species of enchantment evoked below. "Sultry" modifies "light" in the same approximate and transferred sense that couples "warm" with "haze" (20). The second verb in line 21, "refracted," is disturbing. One has an uncomfortable feeling that the poet meant to say "reflected," which is a better alternative to "absorbed" and represents a function possible to a non-translucent medium. Still, the unabridged dictionary (favorite reading of Eliot's) gives "refract" as an obsolete synonym for "reflect." Is this accident or conscious archaism like the spelling in the "daunsinge" piece to follow?

"The dahlias sleep in the empty silence" (22) qualifies as a "perfect line," in which tone, image, rhythm, vowel gradation and transitional consonants contribute to maximum effect within startling economy of compass. "Wait for the early owl" (23) is an admirable companion, giving the same rhythmic satisfaction as "dark in the afternoon" (15) after "Shuttered with branches" (which "sleep in the empty silence" has slightly modified by the insertion of the adjective as additional rhythmic unit) and arousing expectancy so soon to be fulfilled

24   In that open field
25 If you do not come too close, if you do not
                 come too close,
26 On a Summer midnight, you can hear the music
27 Of the weak pipe and the little drum
28 And see them dancing around the bonfire

The "open field" here takes on full significance, appreciated with the cautionary remoteness of 25, which at once places the activities of which the field is the scene in the realm of the ultra-sensory shared by the children in the foliage and the garden presences. The capitalized "Summer" and the hour of midnight, the diminutives "weak" and "little," the "dancing around the bonfire," add up to an impression of Midsummer fairy ring which would vanish were the profane beholder detected. With the complete absence of incongruity typical of dreams the wee folk become Tudor rustics "Lifting heavy feet in clumsy shoes" (37) whose life rhythms, close to the earth and its seasons, their "daunsinge," as Sir Thomas Eliot tells us, mirrors.

29 The association of man and woman
30 In daunsinge, signifying matrimonie—
31 A dignified and commodious sacrament.
32 Two and two, necessarye coniunction,
33 Holding eche other by the hand or the arm
34 Whiche betokeneth concorde. Round and round the
      fire
35 Leaping through the flames, or joined in circles,

36 Rustically solemn or in rustic laughter
37 Lifting heavy feet in clumsy shoes,
38 Earth feet, loam feet, lifted in country mirth
39 Mirth of those long since under earth
40 Nourishing the corn. Keeping time,
41 Keeping the rhythm in their dancing
42 As in their living in the living seasons
43 The time of the seasons and the constellations
44 The time of milking and the time of harvest
45 The time of the coupling of man and woman
46 And that of beasts. Feet rising and falling.
47 Eating and drinking. Dung and death.

After the interpolated lines from the *Boke named the Gouvernour* the syntax breaks down. Prepositions, participles and gerunds maintain the cycles until the rhythmically spent "feet rising and falling./Eating and drinking. Dung and death" (46-47). The omission of grammatically cohesive structural features makes all the greater the demands on sound and rhetoric to provide an organizing principle and prevent disintegration. We find therefore a kind of chain-stitched parataxis in which there is always some element common to adjacent units. Thus sound and sense bind "round" and "joined," "fire" and "flames," respectively (34-35); "Round"-"round" is remembered in "Rustically"-"rustic" (36) while "Leaping" (35) leads into "laughter" (36) and "Lifting" (37); "Lifting...feet" becomes "feet, lifted" (38), "Earth...mirth" is balanced by "Mirth...earth" (39); "Nourishing the corn" recalls the detritus of stalk and leaf which in line 8 accompanied "Bone of man and beast," of "those long since under earth" (39); "Keeping" binds 40 and 41, "in their," 41 and 42, "seasons," 42 and 43, "The time of," 43, 44 and 45; 46 contains "of beasts" as modifier of "coupling" parallel to "of man and woman" (45) (nor need we read in this conjunction the degradation some have seen of the "dignified and commodious sacrament"); "man and... beast," "rising and falling" realte to the earlier "Houses" cycle (2-8), as do the equally earthbound "Eating and drinking. Dung and death."

With 48 the dream-vision is over:

48   Dawn points, and another day
49 Prepares for heat and silence. Out at sea
                        the dawn wind
50 Wrinkles and slides. I am here
51 Or there, or elsewhere. In my beginning.

The change of tone and image is reflected in the altered structure. Three full sentences and a fragment of the refrain are so placed as to set up an undertow against the natural line movement. "Dawn" does not "come" or "rise" or "break," but "points," perhaps meaning "is on the point of opening" (marked "medical" in the unabridged!) or "indicates direction" (as the "lane insist[ed]"). But it seems unnecessary to mine for ambiguities in a word with which we are instinctively satisfied in this place. The "heat and silence" for which the new day prepares harks back to 19-22. East Coker may well look seaward if it was the point of departure for the emigrant Eliots of the seventeenth century. If "wrinkles and slides" describe the intransitive occupation of the "dawn wind" we may believe the scientific explicator who applies these verbs in detail to the behavior of shifting masses of air as they are affected by temperature and pressure changes of early morning.[3] A simpler reading refers the verbs to the observable effect of the wind on the water. The "I" that universalizes the experience as "here" (present), "Or there" (the past of the dancers in the field), "or elsewhere" (unknown or unspecified as befits the future) seems by the repeated first half of the motto to identify self with the rising and falling destinies of the ancestral race and all its progeny.

The first part of Section II is very like the corresponding portion of *Burnt Norton*, from the rhymed octosyllabics to the astronomical imagery. It is interesting that the cosmic chaos should be rendered by verse of such innocent regularity. Perhaps there is a bit of Blake in the background.

52 What is the late November doing
53 With the disturbance of the spring
54 And creatures of the summer heat,
55 And snowdrops writhing under feet
56 And hollyhocks that aim too high
57 Red into grey and tumble down

58 Late roses filled with early snow?
59 Thunder rolled by the rolling stars
60 Simulates triumphal cars
61 Deployed in constellated wars
62 Scorpion fights against the Sun
63 Until the Sun and Moon go down
64 Comets weep and Leonids fly
65 Hunt the heavens and the plains
66 Whirled in a vortex that shall bring
67 The world to that destructive fire
68 Which burns before the ice-cap reigns.

The whole trend of the diction is toward personification: "the late November" seems answerable for its usurpation of "the disturbance of the spring;" snowdrops writhe, hollyhocks aspire and fall, thunder pretends to be something other than itself. Syntactically this out of season thunder storm can account for the heavenly upheaval enlarged upon in the latter half of the passage. In the absence of punctuation we can consider "Scorpion fights..." (62) as beginning not a new sentence but a relative clause (with pronoun suppressed) modifying the "constellated wars" in which the simulated cars are deployed. Pursuing this rationalization, "Until the Sun..." (63) is an adverbial clause with several members and modifies "fights" (62)—until "Comets weep" (admirable as metaphor and in keeping with the personification noted as characteristic), until "Leonids fly" (as regularly recurring November showers of shooting stars) and "Hunt the heavens and the plains" (appropriate employment for beings of leonine origin) and are "Whirled in a vortex" at the end of the world, sidereal universe and all.

The rhetorical and metrical aspects of the passage offer little complication. The two "W" lines, 52-53, form an interrogative unit in which the natural voice inflections are called into play with no less sureness than delicacy. The first halves of the lines correspond exactly:

Whāt ĭš thĕ lāte... / Wĭth thĕ dĭstūrb-

while

(-)
...Nŏvēmbĕr dōĭŋg / ...-ănce of thĕ sprīng —

convert the slight difference in pitch and vowel placement into rhythmic ingredients of a somewhat harassed question. For all practical purposes this first couplet does not rhyme.

54-56 exhibit a parallel semi-structure and complete adherence to the basic iambic tetrameter which the seventeen lines under discussion depart from oftener than they conform to. Again the strict resemblance is confined to the first halves of the lines, in each case "And" plus plural noun. The nouns are modified in turn by a prepositional phrase, a participial phrase and a relative clause. The last modifier having attained the quasi-independence of the finite verb, "aim," branches into a second, "tumble," whose adverb, "down," later places "Sun and Moon" (63) as well as "Hollyhocks." The color words—this is the sole occurrence of "red" in all four of the *Quartets,* and the only other appearance of "grey" is in the first section of the same one, "grey stone" (21)—may be an impressionistic picture of the red blooms reaching into the grey November sky (not unlike the sleeping dahlias [23] in the line next to the "grey stone") or merely red petals fading into purplish-grey at their base. The balanced antithesis, "Late roses filled with early snow" (58), is horticulturally the least preposterous of the flower lines. In this respect their order is descending. Hollyhocks (56) may be among the "creatures of the summer heat" that can be beguiled by a late St. Martin's summer, but snowdrops (55) are rather an apparition of the "midwinter spring" of *Little Gidding.* We are thus introduced into the midst of the disordered seasons with their rhythms as sadly disrupted (as far as *cultivated* nature—the flowers are all garden varieties—is concerned) as are those of constellations, no longer (as in 43) a peaceful mirroring of a harmonious microcosm.

"Down" (57) has no rhyme but is repeated in 63, while 64, "fly," rhymes with "high" in 56. "Snow" (58) is also unrhymed but the eye is caught by the rearrangement of the three letters it has in common with "down" just above (as is the case in the adjacent "Simulates triumphal" two lines later) and the vowel is supported by "roses" as well as by the onomatopoeic "rolled"-"rolling" in the "Thunder" line (59). "Wars" (61) as eye rhyme after "stars"-"cars" prepares for the initial "Scorpion" (62) to resist the entrance of the sun into the "late November" terrain of the zodiac. The "airish beasts" are active in the reeling welkin. So were man and woman dancing "Round and round the fire / ... joined in circles" (34-35).

A close series of vowel-n words unites 62 and 63— "Scorpion fights against the Sun / Until the Sun and Moon go down"—but the tonal impression is not single. "Fights" is the principal intrusion and looks to "fly" (64) and "fire" (67) while "against" more quietly anticipates "plains" (65) and "reigns" (68). Little alliterations like "Hunt the heavens" (65) and "burns before" (68) help to restore the feeling of the line as self-contained unit. The "Whirled"—"world" combination we have seen before, though not so intimate, in *Burnt Norton* III. The capitalization of Sun and Moon is a further instance of the tendency toward personification already noted as distinguishing this passage.

Then we dismiss the "periphrastic study in a wornout poetical fashion" (70) for a freer-cadenced continuation of the "wrestle / With words and meanings" (71-72). Attention is focussed not on the function of words—section V is as before devoted to that problem—but on the loss to wisdom of the misvaluing of expereince. We proceed by questions whose cumulative phrases (including the semi-appositional "serenity" and "wisdom" groups appearing [79-82] after the interrogation point) emphasize the futility of surface knowledge and pat formulae in the face of the intense reality and besetting illusion that together confront the human spirit. The syntactic development is misleadingly casual, the diction studiously tentative:

69 That was a way of putting it—not very satisfactory:
70 A periphrastic study in a worn-out poetical fashion
71 Leaving one still with the intolerable wrestle
72 With words and meanings. The poetry does not matter.
73 It was not (to start again) what one had expected.

Some rhetorical sweep is admitted into the next lines with their much modified and delayed key nouns, "age" and "elders" (76 and 77), with their rhythmically effective repetitions "long looked forward to,/Long hoped for" (74-75), "deceived us/Or deceived themselves" (76-77), and the word play of "receipt for deceit" (75).

> 74 What was to be the value of the long looked
>   forward to,
> 75 Long hoped for calm, the autumnal serenity
> 76 And the wisdom of age? Had they deceived us
> 77 Or deceived themselves, the quiet-voiced elders,
> 78 Bequeathing us merely a receipt for deceit?

Lines 79-82 middle are carefully balanced with as carefully admitted variety, and this where we have by now come to expect it, in the second half of the line.

> 79 The serenity only a deliberate hebetude,
> 80 The wisdom only the knowledge of dead secrets
> 81 Useless in the darkness into which they peered
> 82 Or from which they turned their eyes.

Indefinite article and preceding adjective qualify "hebetude;" definite article and following prepositional phrase limit "knowledge." From the latter word depends a chain of modifying words and phrases ending in the alternatives which balance the second half of 81 against the first half of 82: the "knowledge" that masquerades as wisdom is "Useless" in the kind of darkness the soul suffers, where living mysteries outrank "dead secrets," which is as closed to peering curiosity as to averted gaze.

The answer to the value question begun in 74 picks up the wisdom-as-knowledge note and continues from there. It looks therefore as though wisdom's partner, "serenity" (they are so paired in 75-76 and 79-80), were sufficiently disposed of by its unmasking as "hebetude." A hint of conflict arises with its original adjective, "autumnal," since the conditions exemplified in the November passage a few lines earlier were of the most unserene acuity. We hardly look for this kind of irony here, but we can read beneath "quiet-voiced" (77) flanked as it is by "deceived" (76-77) and "deceit" (78) the sinister implications possible to "smooth-tongued" or "soft-spoken." "Receipt" (78) can mean "recipe" or "acknowledgement of payment received;" the bequest in either case is bitter, and like the "deliberate hebetude" heavy with the refusals of *Gerontion.*

Exaggeration is avoided in the brief assessment:

82   There is, it seems to us,
83 At best, only a limited value
84 In the knowledge derived from experience.

The diagnosis proceeds with renewed assurance,

85 The knowledge imposes a pattern, and falsifies,
86 For the pattern is new in every moment
87 And every moment is a new and shocking
88 Valuation of all we have been.

The first "pattern," external form and imposed from without, the product of short-ranged temporal experience and mechanical repetition, is contrasted with the liberating "pattern" that is the informing principle and preserver of what is viable in "every moment" of purified awareness, of "new and shocking / Valuation," of time past in the light of the eternal present. The "limited value" of the knowledge derived deductively from experience rather than intuited in experience lies in its negative role of disabusing us (even while it falsifies) of past errors whose force is long since spent.

88   We are only undeceived
89 Of that which, deceiving, could no longer harm.

After the relaxation of rhetoric in "There is, it seems to us, / At best, only a limited value" (82-83), where, however, the apologetic parentheses indicate a species of intellectual tension, we notice a resumption of "technique" in the peculiar word-threading occasionally resorted to (as in 37 ff.):

84 knowledge
85 knowledge   pattern
86 pattern   new   moment
87 moment   new

then

88   undeceived
89 deceiving

A syntactically unattached *Inferno* echo resets the scene:

90 In the middle, not only in the middle of the way

91 But all the way, in a dark wood, in a bramble,
92 On the edge of a grimpen, where is no secure
    foothold,
93 And menaced by monsters, fancy lights,
94 Risking enchantment.

Is it "we" who are in the treacherous terrain and the darkness of the useless secrets, "we" in the middle of the way, as well as the deceived or deceiving elders, who are threatened by that which still has power to harm? If one seeks for these symbols a local habitation and a name, Dartmoor in Devon, west of Somerset (East Coker's county), has its ancient forest and surviving dwarf oak tracts, the "Great Grimpen Mire"[4] with its "fancy lights" of marshy exhalation, its overtones of bloody history and grim fiction. Within the poem we find other relations: the foreboding of the octosyllabic passage with its "destructive fire" (67); the chimera in the desert toward the end of *Burnt Norton*; the very different "enchantment" of the "Summer midnight" (26).

There is a new intensity in the rhythm-phrase, "edge of a grimpen" (92), "menaced by monsters" (93), "risking enchantment" (94), as it moves progressively nearer the beginning of the line. (This dactyl-trochee combination is not uncommon—"Had they deceived us" [76], "quiet-voiced elders" [77], "limited value" [83]—but at the end of the line, as in these last examples, it tends to assume the stately finality of the dactyl-spondee close of the classical hexameter and its urgency is obscured.) The same phrases, it will be noted, contain four, three and two words respectively (and, if the compound is split, the same decrease in word count characterizes the examples in the last parenthesis). It is as though the mounting excitement had succeeded in crystallizing what was looseness and hesitancy at the beginning of the pseudo-sentence which may almost be said to stutter:

| 90 | In the | | in the | |
| 91 | | in a | | in a |

| 90 | | middle | | middle | way |
| 91 | | way | | | |

Letter patterns are discernible though not prominent: "way"-"way"-"wood"-"where," "middle"-"middle"-"br*a*mble"-

"grimpen"-"menaced"-"monsters." The m-group incidentally illustrates the prevalence in this place of two-syllabled words accenting the first.

A new (and genuine) sentence opens with the even-paced monosyllables of the second half of 94:

94   Do not let me hear
95 Of the wisdom of old men, but rather of their folly
96 Their fear of fear and frenzy, their fear of
    possession,
97 Of belonging to another, or to others, or to God.

Half-lines emerge again as rhetorical units, in 95 of contrast, in 96 of amplification. In the latter attention is caught at once by the triple "fear," the first and third identical in function and modifier, the second by its duplication of sound making all the more striking its role as objective genitive. This in turn highlights the "of" series in which we find three different relationships expressed by the same preposition: "hear/Of" (twice, with the verb understood in the second instance), "fear of" (twice expressed, as if to make sure the line-apart rhyme is felt, and once more without repetition of "fear"), and the simple possessive, "wisdom of old men," inserted between the examples of the first type. The succession of objects of the last "of's" is interesting: "fear and frenzy," "possession" (96), "belonging" (97). "Possession" with its dual connotation dovetails into both "frenzy" and "belonging" and brings about a remarkable transition from one to the other diametrically opposed state. Line 97 continues the ascent with three degrees of self-giving whose naming is their only description with such apparent artlessness of diction that we are surprised to observe that every one of the ten simple words contains an "o". There is pattern in the phonetic series [ʌ] [ɔː] [u] thrice repeated and the final [ɒ], and a kind of counterpoint to this in the word grouping which the sense enforces, [ʌ] [ɔː] [u] [v], [ɔː] [u] [ʌ], [ɔː] [u] [ɒ]. The suppression of the third "fear" suggests a pause before "Of belonging." With this last "Of" we leave behind the "f's" which, voiced or unvoiced, played such a large part in the sound complexion of 95-96: "Of"-"of"-"of"-"folly"-"fear of fear"-"frenzy"-"fear of."

The illusory "wisdom" of 76, 80 and 95 is dismissed with

the discovery of 98-99, a consequence of the "belonging" of 97.

98 The only wisdom we can hope to acquire
99 Is the wisdom of humility: humility is endless.

There is a note of humility in "we can hope to acquire," and the seemingly tentative

98 wisdom
99 wisdom   humility   humility

which reverses the key-word scheme noted (above, p. 54) of 90-91 brings us at last to the quiet assurance of "endless" with all it evoked as supra-temporal security.

The spaced and indented[5] single lines with which the section closes

100 The houses are all gone under the sea.

101 The dancer are all gone under the hill.

remind us that other things are not endless—the houses and dancers of section I "are all gone," "under the sea"[6] whence "the dawn wind" rises, "under the hill" where they nourish the corn—but even these are part of a life cycle larger than they wherein resurrections in deed or in symbol are always before us.

The first line of section III picks up the cry, "all gone," but with the temper and direction of section III of *Burnt Norton*. The "dim light" of the earlier poem has deepened inescapably; its emptiness is more complete, and the contrast between the two kinds of emptiness is clearer. There is a heavier irony and in *East Coker* it is carried by the six-line catalogue of the worldly great (with the astronomical inclusion significantly capitalized and recalling the cosmic chaos of the first part of section II). Whatever of Milton or Whitman we hear in these and the opening lines adds to their impact.

102 O dark dark dark. They all go into the dark,
103 The vacant interstellar spaces, the vacant into the
        vacant,
104 The captains, merchant bankers, eminent men of
        letters,

105 The generous patrons of art, the statesmen and the rulers,
106 Distinguished civil servants, chairmen of many committees,
107 Industrial lords and petty contractors, all go into the dark,
108 And dark the Sun and Moon, and the Almanach de Gotha
109 And the Stock Exchange Gazette, the Directory of Directors,
110 And cold the sense and lost the motive of action.
111 And we all go with them, into the silent funeral,
112 Nobody's funeral, for there is no one to bury.

The triply apostrophized "dark"—one is struck by the recurrent three's in Eliot's patterns, as well as by his retention of the poetic "o"[7]—is to be the arena of the entire action of this part of the poem. It is equated with the "vacant interstellar spaces," and "They" who enter it are also called vacant, and immediately named as the mighty and influential, the respected and feared in a society of "limited value[s]." With the "Sun and Moon" are eclipsed the observers and their findings in the financial firmament overspreading the world scene where what is human in sense and motive is chilled into quiescence and the shattered mechanism of a Newtonian universe disintegrates further in magnate-made warfare. The near annihilation of "Nobody's funeral" represents the nadir of societal collapse, from which rises like the phoenix the psalmodic cry of the individual seeking redemption:

113 I said to my soul, be still, and let the dark come upon you
114 Which shall be the darkness of God.

A salient feature of this passage is its strenuous rhythm. Caesural commas break the long six-stress lines, exceptions to which are now fewer. There is a Kiplingesque beat in the roll call, or perhaps an ironic echo of "Into the valley of death rode the six hundred."

Except for the vowel contrast between the first two lines,

102 dark dark dark   dark
103 vacant   spaces   vacant   vacant,

there does not seem to be any calculated sound scheme. The rhythm is determined by the predominantly disyllabic characters and their more varied modifiers. The first half of 104 and the second half of 105 are structurally close and rhythmically identical: "The captains, merchant bankers, / ... the statesmen and the rulers." Their other halves," ... eminent men of letters, / The generous patrons of art," but for the gratuitous "The" and the reversal of syllable distribution on either side of the "of's," correspond exactly. The resulting figure is an intricate double chiasmus, rhythmic within structural-rhythmic. 106 we can regard alone—as rhythmical phrase repeated with embellishment (the two extra slack syllables making dactyls of "chairmen of many committees")—or in relation to the two preceding lines—as returning to the syntactical order of 104 which 105 had reversed, but introducing a slight variation in its first half with the single noun doubly modified. The "Industrial lords and petty contractors" expand the first half of 107 but arithmetically do not exceed the syllable count established by earlier adjective (three)-noun (two) pairs—it is having both members modified that tips the balance. Its second half, "all go into the dark," seems shorter; it can be read as two-stressed, giving 107 the four-two division of 103 while at the same time it echoes the refrain of 102. There is a certain symmetry in 106-109, turning on the "dark" half-lines, the last of 107 and the first of 108, but in 108-109 "dark" has become an adjective of quality instead of a noun of place (or state). As applicable to celestial bodies as to mundane organs of information, it denotes absence of warmth as well as deprivation of light; hence in " cold the sense and lost the motive" (110) we find a logical development, the more cogent for the preservation of the word order of "dark the Sun [etc.]." The initial "And" further binds 108-111. "Into the silent funeral" (111) resembles in line position and adverbial connection with another "go" the earlier phrases "into the dark" (102-107), "into the vacant" (103). The "silent funeral" (unrelieved even by a "crying shadow"), "Nobody's funeral," is indeed dark and vacant. Is it a case of "Let the dead bury the dead," of the insubstantial "unhealthy souls" blown like leaves by the "cold wind" of *Burnt Norton* III, unreposeful because unburied save in the rubble that confounded "Men and bits of paper" ("The captains, merchant bankers, [etc.]" and "the Almanach de Gotha,/And the Stock Exchange Gazette, the Directory of Directors")?

The way in which the other darkness, "the darkness of God," should come upon one is expressed by a three-fold image, first:

114   As, in a theatre,
115 The lights are extinguished, for the scene to be changed
116 With a hollow rumble of wings, with a movement of darkness on darkness,
117 And we know that the hills and the trees, the distant panorama
118 And the bold imposing façade are all being rolled away—

116-118 represent a strong rhythmic return to the measure of 104 ff. In the "hollow rumble of wings" we hear a simulated thunder; here "darkness" moves on "darkness" as an active force. With the change of scene, then, comes a change of roles. There is a hint of tautology in "distant panorama" and in "bold imposing" and "imposing façade," a possible redundancy in "the hills and trees, the distant panorama." But this superfluity is "all being rolled away" as the seeming with the sensible gives place to the purifying darkness.

The next image returns with insistence to the "strained time-ridden faces" of *Burnt Norton* III.[8]

119 Or as, when an underground train, in the tube, stops too long between stations
120 And the conversation rises and slowly fades into silence
121 And you see behind every face the mental emptiness deepen
122 Leaving only the growing terror of nothing to think about;

The meter of the first three lines especially recalls the hexameters of *Evangeline* rather than their classical originals. (Eliot by his habitual and recognized use of literary echoes leaves himself open to the most far-fetched attributions, but by his own admission[9] no reader-made associations are barred.)

On the significance as image of the London underground railway a commentator in *MLN* has an interesting remark. Informing us that the core of the system is the "Inner Circle," "a line which has no terminus," and pointing out that "of a circle it is always true to say, 'In my beginning is my end,'" he continues: "Stripped of its mundane associations, in fact, the Inner Circle can be conceived as a symbol of almost Dantesque power, and one which is so appropriate to the theme of the *Quartets* that it is difficult to escape from the conclusion that it must form one of the basic images of the poem."[10]

The first image emphasizes darkness and movement, the second, vacancy and inertness—the train "stops too long" (119), the conversation "fades into silence" (120). That "growing terror" (122) should be the end-product of "mental emptiness" (121) perhaps finds greater confirmation in our mental hospitals than in any logic inherent in the language of this syntactically detached simile.

The third image is not altogether distinct from the second:

> 123   Or when, under ether, the mind is conscious but
>   conscious of nothing—

The dash at the end of 118 finds a counterpart only here, after 123. If consistency of punctuation is at all indicative it points to a partial inclusion at least of the etherized mind with the minds otherwise evacuated. The introductory "As" (114), "Or as" (119) also support this grouping. The "when" in both 119 and 123 seems to convey parallel subordination not shared by any member of the 114-118 word group, whose coordinate "lights are extinguished" and "we know" are immediately governed only by the "As" of doubtful function. On the other hand, the terminal "rolled away" (118) of the first simile is metrically balanced by one of the two readings possible to "think about" (122), a circumstance arguing that the latter words also end a rhetorical unit. Read differently, of course, "nothing to think about" is closer to "emptiness deepen" (121), "fades into silence" (120) and "long between stations" (119), but even so the extra syllable with

its secondary stress carries a suggestion of finality to which
the semi-colon bears independent witness. Can we say that
the doubtful fusion is in itself a factor contributing to the
effect of scene dissolving into new half-realized scene?

With "conscious of nothing" (123) (once its association
with "nothing to think about" [122] is left behind) we are
disposed to credit the readiness of soul which will wait in its
destitution, "without hope" (124), "without love" (125),
"without thought" (128) until its passive purification shall
issue in transforming union.

124 I said to my soul, be still, and wait without hope
125 For hope would be hope for the wrong thing; wait
without love
126 For love would be love of the wrong thing; there is
yet faith
127 But the faith and the love and the hope are all in the
waiting.
128 Wait without thought, for you are not ready for
thought:
129 So the darkness shall be the light, and the stillness
the dancing.

The first half of 124 is identical with that of 113. The
earlier imperative introduced the "darkness of God" with
three similes from contexts whose very remoteness
suggested the difficulty of describing the soul's submission to
it. Here the soul is bidden embrace a three-fold deprivation
by waiting in faith, a discipline akin rather to the night of the
spirit (which in St. John of the Cross follows the night of the
senses to which the reactions of 114ff. might be considered
as approximating) than to the Quietist abstention from acts
to which it is sometimes likened. The compression of 124ff.
is appropriately greater than that of the companion lines
above, and is somewhat paradoxically rendered by the
patterned repetitions which alter little more than the key
nouns in 125-126. After the summary line 127 we return in
128 to the "wait"-clause and "for"-clause whose line positions
here seem, largely through the resulting rhythmic modification, to alter the relationship set up in 124-126. 129
represents whatever degree of resolution and fulfillment can
be looked for at this stage. That this is anticipation the "shall

be" tells us, but a new assurance is discernible in the rest of
the section, and when the poet proposes to "say it again"
(136) his restatement has an authority born of experience on
a level a little deeper (or to the percipient a little more
comprehensible) than the ineffable awareness of *Burnt
Norton's* garden (to which 132 looks back) and the felt but
incompletely plumbed eternal "still point" where "the dance
is" (*BN* 65).

> 130   Whisper of running streams, and winter light-
> ning.
> 131 The wild thyme unseen and the wild strawberry,
> 132 The laughter in the garden, echoed ecstasy
> 133 Not lost, but requiring, pointing to the agony
> 134 Of death and birth.

The likeness of these few lines to *Burnt Norton* IV is at
once apparent, but their affinities are farther-reaching. The
"running streams" with the "wild thyme" and the "wild
strawberry" lead us out of the strictly cultivated landscape in
which Eliot has seemed most at home. The "winter
lightning" recalls the confused seasons of section II. The at
first delicate "w" alliteration accompanied in 130 by short "i"
and in 131 resouding in the crescendo of the identical "wild"
with the diphthong duplicated in "thyme" binds 130 and 131,
as does the phrasal structure: substantive group-and-
substantive group. (The variation here, contrary to Eliot's
practice in similar pairings elsewhere,[11] is in the first halves
of the lines, where however the syntactically different
modifiers show a common sound-scheme: "*running streams*"-
"*unseen*;" the second halves are substantially equivalent in
syntactical make-up and syllable count, a British strawberry
being disyllabic.) The punctuation, though—a full stop after
"lightning"—would tend to keep them apart if its significance
were grammatical. That it is employed chiefly to time the
pause at the end of line 130 with relation to those after 131
(comma) and the rest (no end punctuation until the period
closing the rhetorical unit with the truncated line 134) we
may assume from the absence in 130-134 of any finite verb
which could weld the substantive elements into a complete
sentence.

The recapitulation and interweaving of motives reaches a

peak of allusiveness in 131-132. Wild thyme is traditionally associated with the midsummer midnight fairy revels glimpsed momentarily in section I. In 131 for the first time we deal consciously with scents, always evocative but perhaps especially so in the case of thyme and wild strawberry with their potential wealth of childhood associations. "Unseen" once applied to the laughing children, and the easy transference strengthens our sense of assembling pattern. The remembered laughter is "echoed ecstasy" (the more poignant therefore is the deprivation of 139—"You must go by a way wherein there is no ecstasy"), "requiring," seeking again, the life-through-death that has been so insistent a theme throughout the poem and that has just been imaged in the winter-in-summer, winter-and-summer lines 130 and 131 whose utter naturalness of symbolism debars a charge of triteness—here we see Eliot working within the tradition but with a sophistication of selectivity which gives his treatment the freshness of originality. The "running streams" need no other justification than their inherent rebirth symbolism; it would be folly to relate them to the mighty river of *The Dry Salvages* for the sake of linking "winter lightning" to *Little Gidding's* "Midwinter spring," although this passage may certainly be regarded as one of the milestones of the *Quartets*, where we look forward and backward and gather our forces for new discoveries.

135   You say I am repeating
136 Something I have said before. I shall say it again.
137 Shall I say it again? In order to arrive there,
138 To arrive where you are, to get from where you are not,
139 You must go by a way wherein there is no ecstasy.
140 In order to arrive at what you do not know
141   You must go by a way which is the way of ignorance.
142 In order to possess what you do not possess
143   You must go by the way of dispossession.
144 In order to arrive at what you are not
145   You must go through the way in which you are not.

146 And what you do not know is the only thing you
     know
147 And what you own is what you do not own
148 And where you are is where you are not.

Again the ritual chant and solemn dance, and the slow
strokes that teach detachment—we will remember these precepts when in *LG* I (21ff., 41ff.) they are confirmed by example. Here the diction is unadorned, as nearly colorless as all
the drab monosyllables can make it. The syntax is simple in
its uniformity although the corresponding units reveal the
complexity that arises when a clause must serve for the word
one cannot find (like Robert Frost's definition of home as
"where, when you have to go there, they have to take you
in"[12]—a kindred New England strain?). The rhetoric is in the
scriptural ring of the double anaphora (which the indentation
emphasizes), "In order to...," "You must go...," and the
final triplet, "and wh-," where the least of copulatives makes
paradoxes of the mutually cancelling noun clauses. The order
is still: positive is negative—In my beginning is my end.

Section IV consists of five five-line stanzas rhymed
$a_4b_4a_4b_5b_6$. The rhymes, except "hospital"—"shall" (159, 161)
and "food"—"blood"—"good" (171, 173, 174), are exact and
the exceptions quite traditional. The "numbers" too are regular except for the not unexpected grace note of "by the"
(160).

149 The wounded surgeon plies the steel
150 That questions the distempered part;
151 Beneath the bleeding hands we feel
152 The sharp compassion of the healer's art
153 Resolving the enigma of the fever chart.

154 [13]Our only health is the disease
155 If we obey the dying nurse
156 Whose constant care is not to please
157 But to remind of our, and Adam's curse,
158 And that, to be restored, our sickness must grow
     worse.

159   The whole earth is our hospital
160 Endowed by the ruined millionaire,
161 Wherein, if we do well, we shall

162 Die of the absolute paternal care
163 That will not leave us, but prevents us everywhere.

164   The chill ascends from feet to knees
165 The fever sings in mental wires.
166 If to be warmed, then I must freeze
167 And quake in frigid purgatorial fires
168 Of which the flame is roses, and the smoke is briars.

169   The dripping blood our only drink,
170 The bloody flesh our only food:
171 In spite of which we like to think
172 That we are sound, substantial flesh and blood—
173 Again, in spite of that, we call this Friday good.

This section has proved a fertile field for interpretive comment and "metaphysical" identification.[14] It yields quite as much enrichment to a tentative investigation of the techniques it brings to the thematic development which is here the most explicitly Christian we have so far encountered.

With syntax as starting point we notice a change from the thoroughly organized "surgeon," "nurse" and "hospital" stanzas—each a single complete sentence—in the elliptical purgatory and Good Friday stanzas. The rhetoric, if we except the oxymoron of the "frigid...fires" (167) and the frequent small alliterations, is integral with the stanzaic structure. Thus the first and second line of each stanza are closely related to each other and in some way separated from the three remaining lines which in turn constitute a unit. In 149-150, 154-155 and 159-160 the second line of the pair is a grammatical modifier of the first or of an elment in it; the pairs 164-165 and 169-170 are syntactically parallel. Similarly 151-153, 156-158 and 161-163 form closer sequences than do 166-168 (where the break is the introduction of the totally new image in the last line) and 171-173 (where the punctuation prepares us for the finality of the concluding observation).

The diction comes to new life in its roots and ramifications—"questions" (150) for "probes," "prevents" (163) for "anticipates"—and suggests relationships of likeness and contrast which strengthen the internal unity of the poem. "Distempered" affords such a contrast, almost by pun. We think of the tempered steel of God-sent, God-suffered pain whose "sharp compassion" rights our disorder, while our appreciation has something in it of the Apostle Thomas' if we read aright the hint of transitive in "feel" conjoined with "bleeding hands" (151). (And the preposition is "Beneath," not "behind.")

In the next stanza, the reference to the Church Militant alludes to its ending with time and possibly hints at internal weakness, but relentless effort as well. The word order may imply deliberately unpleasing persistence on the part of the "dying nurse." Does the "If" (155) veil a reservation? The question is pertinent in view of the sequence "health is...disease/If..." rather than the reverse.

A similar inversion of expected word order occurs in the "hospital" stanza. It reads not "we shall do well if we die..." but "if we do well, we shall/Die..." (161-162). When one dies "of" something the "of" is clearly causal. We may unravel this to "Death (as rebirth) through Divine Providence is the reward of well-doing," as the *felix culpa* is the endowment of the "ruined millionaire." And there are echoes of "Go ye into the whole world..." and "I will be with you all days."

"The chill ascends..." and "fever sings..." (164-165) in a few telling strokes bring before us not only the physical aspects of dying but its ironic parody of the exuberant life of the "trilling wire in the blood" (*BN* 51) and its "Ascen[t] to summer" in the ordered macrocosm whose reconciliations *EC* II made void. "If [I am] to be warmed, then I must freeze" (166) and the two following lines compose one of the most startling syntheses of the entire poem, implying the gamut of images of the *Divine Comedy* from the hell of ice to the rose of light.

If we began with Herbert we end with Crashaw or one of the emblem poets. Calvary and the Eucharist vividly confront us in 169-170, albeit solely under the aspect of Viaticum (judging from the tenor of the preceding stanza and from "In spite of which" introducing the assumption of 172). Sacramental theology underlies the ironic use of "substantial" as applied to the "flesh and blood" of debilitated humanity which has been demonstrated as hardly "sound" either. The problem of assigning antecedents, simple for "which" in 171 referring clearly to the facts designated by 169-170, is less so for "that" in 173. With *hic* versus *ille* in mind we look before 171-172 to the more remote reference of 169-170, selecting as focus Our Lord's Passion, our participation in the fruits of which justifies the final epithet "good."

Section V returns to the consideration of words which so troubled the poet in *BN* V.

174 So here I am, in the middle way, having had twenty years—
175 Twenty years largely wasted, the years of *l'entre deux guerres*—
176 Trying to learn to use words, and every attempt
177 Is a wholly new start, and a different kind of failure
178 Because one has only learnt to get the better of words
179 For the thing one no longer has to say, or the way in which
180 One is no longer disposed to say it.

With this resumption of the "intolerable wrestle / With words and meanings" (*EC* 71-72) by one "in the middle way" (174) we half expect an allusion to the "quiet-voiced elders." These enter a little farther on where however they have become the masters "whom one cannot hope / To emulate" (186-187). The twenty wasted years (wasted, that is, by the Europe of the Almanach de Gotha, by the merchant bankers and industrial lords, by the patrons of art and men of letters, by all those whose destination in section III was the dark and vacant waste of the second World War) were not altogether unproductive from the craftsman's point of view—one wonders whether "words" are not viewed here as tools, "shabby equipment" (182), even more than as medium. As simple communication, an unadorned "way of putting it," in this passage they are most matter-of-fact, and conversationally arranged. Matter and manner, it is said, always just elude the shaping power of words. We are then in the realm of understatement, of yesterday's realizations. The discouraged artist continues with a mildly military analogy:

180   And so each venture
181 Is a new beginning, a raid on the inarticulate
182 With shabby equipment always deteriorating
183 In the general mess of imprecision of feeling,
184 Undisciplined squads of emotion. And what there is
     to conquer
185 By strength and submission, has already been
     discovered
186 Once or twice, or several times, by men whom one
     cannot hope
187 To emulate—but there is no competition—
188 There is only the fight to recover what has been
     lost
189 And found and lost again and again: and now, under
     conditions
190 That seem unpropitious. But perhaps neither gain
     nor loss.
191 For us there is only the trying. The rest is not our
     business.

The words of *Burnt Norton* V were found to "Decay with imprecision" as with an inherent weakness. Here it is their environment which is blamed for their failure, "the general mess of imprecision of feeling" (183). "Undisciplined squads of emotion" (184) can best parallel the "general mess" as the agents abusing the "shabby equipment" of words.

The combined "strength and submission" (185) of the poet as craftsman and artist who both makes and is patient have served some few to discover "what there is to conquer" (184) (not to conquer it). Against increasing odds, "For us there is only the trying." The alternates and repetitions convey a sense of effort as the "fight" for them keeps up the subdued metaphor. "Lost again" (189) and "gain nor loss" (190), the latter in an independently punctuated but verbless *sotto voce*, form perhaps the only sound-device intruding on the monotone of the passage.

The next part returns to the basic four-stress pattern after the longer lines with their tendency to break. As in the corresponding portion of *Burnt Norton* we find the recapitulation by brief touches, often a single word, of the principal thematic strains, and a sudden passage of concretely imaged reminiscence. "Love" reappears after a considerable interval (it was mentioned only for its absence in 125-126) and as before (*BN 166*) seems to have been in the discussion all along. The scope is broader than that of *Burnt Norton*'s conclusion, cumulative with respect to what has gone before and more explicitly looking forward to *The Dry Salvages* and *Little Gidding*.

> 192   Home is where one starts from. As we grow older
> 193 The world becomes stranger, the pattern more complicated
> 194 Of dead and living. Not the intense moment
> 195 Isolated, with no before and after,
> 196 But a lifetime burning in every moment
> 197 And not the lifetime of one man only
> 198 But of old stones that cannot be deciphered.

192 names "the place you would be likely to come from" (*LG* 23), seeming from the next sentence to stress its remembered security. Advancing age is again something of a problem. The world (not the still point at its center), the pattern (that which in 85 experimental knowledge imposed, not that which in *BN* 143 was a means to stillness) grow respectively "stranger" and "more complicated." The first adjective gives us a paradoxical "unfamiliar" and another meaning shared with the second, "harder to understand." The change is of course subjective, taking place as the mind accepting becomes the tester of values. The phrase modifier of "pattern" surprises—not "of death and life," but "Of dead and living." The reference is to persons, the dancers now under the hill and their time-ridden descendants who have lost the secret of their rhythmic living. The syntactically free "intense moment / Isolated" (194-195) (or rather the "lifetime burning" to which it quickly yields) may be identified with the complicated pattern of living (as gerund now), or taken as a kind of cognate accusative with "living" (here also as gerund). The utter simplicity of the timeless moment at the still point is incompatible with patterned complexity. The burning of this lifetime is more that of purgatory than of the hard gem-like flame, and it is common to all, not sparing the generation of the Tudor dancers whose tombstones now yield up no story but that of the yew-tree at the end of *The Dry Salvages* or in *Burnt Norton* IV.

199 There is a time for the evening under starlight,
200 A time for the evening under lamplight
201 (The evening with the photograph album).

Starlight and lamplight lead to the "winter gaslight" (*DS* 14) and bring together the home scenes of the end of *East Coker* and the beginning of *The Dry Salvages*. These are presented without nostalgia but, here especially, as a validation ("There is a time for...") of the starting point which, with or without intimations of immortality, represented a period of purer realization and an approach to truly integral experience. The transition is easy to

202 Love is most nearly itself
203 When here and now cease to matter.

Again the stripping of limitations aspires to an absolute, figured by the closing of the circle of love's self-identification, end and beginning the same.

204 Old men ought to be explorers
205 Here and there does not matter
206 We must be still and still moving
207 Into another intensity
208 For a further union, a deeper communion
209 Through the dark cold and the empty desolation
210 The wave cry, the wind cry, the vast waters
211 Of the petrel and the porpoise.   In my end is my
      beginning.

The abandonment of punctuation in the first few lines of these concluding eight softens the outlines of the reflective cadences. Old men if explorers would have more to bequeath than their "knowledge of dead secrets" (80). "Here and there" must denote singular "place" or imply motion between if the auxiliary "does" is to fit. The accidents of time, place and motion then are relegated beyond consideration in the stillness which progresses only into deeper intensities, via the dark nights into the unitive way. The sea images and the storm bird and the many-symboled dolphin draw us into the next of the *Quartets* while in sound and picture they round out our vision with flow of line and pause and lettering. The sea before the separation of the waters, the sea that swallowed the houses, is before and after puny man. But "the spirit of God moved over the waters" and the void and empty earth brought forth living creatures. And God said, "There shall no more be waters of a flood to destroy all flesh." Truly, "In my end is my beginning."

✌ 3 ✌

The Dry Salvages

THE THIRD *Quartet* opens with a fourteen-line almost pentameter passage. Lines 11-14, though, are clearly four-stressed, and the terminal words of each line seem purposely as un-iambic as possible—except for "intractable" (2) and "implacable" (7) all are accented on the penult syllable.[1] Three of the last four lines end in compounds, "bedroom," "dooryard," "gaslight," whose second elements have greater weight than the final syllables of words like "table" (13), "waiting" (10), "bridges" (5) and the rest. We look in vain for any sonnet-like division—the nearest we come to a true *volta* is the shift in tense and rhythm that distinguishes 11-14.

1 I do not know much about gods; but I think that the river

2 Is a strong brown god—sullen, untamed and intractable,

3 Patient to some degree, at first recognised as a frontier;

4 Useful, untrustworthy, as a conveyor of commerce;

5 Then only a problem confronting the builder of bridges.

6 The problem once solved, the brown god is almost forgotten

7 By the dwellers in cities—ever, however, implac-able,

8 Keeping his seasons and rages, destroyer, reminder

9 Of what men choose to forget. Unhonoured, unpropitiated

10 By worshippers of the machine, but waiting, watching and waiting.

11 His rhythm was present in the nursery bedroom,
12 In the rank ailanthus of the April dooryard,
13 In the smell of grapes on the autumn table,
14 And the evening circle in the winter gaslight.

One interesting feature of the diction is the unusual percentage of negative adjectives (or participles): "untamed," "intractable" (2), "untrustworthy" (4), "implacable" (7), "Unhonoured, unpropitiated" (9). These are all applied to the river which is also "strong," "brown" and "sullen" (2) and secondarily "Patient," "Useful," and "almost forgotten" (3, 4, 6). The modifiers in the latter group thus isolated seem irreverently mule-like. We are actually, though, not far from the animal in the hint of primitive forces under the uncertain control of reason and civilization, while the demonstration of power unleashed in the hinted Mississippi flood is aptly imaged in the initial apotheosis. The surging waters are felt in the onomatopoeic rhythm in which the familiar beat of terminal phrases like "builder of bridges" (5), "conveyor of commerce" (4) takes on a new aspect of advance and recession. The alliteration, of brief compass as in the last examples, or spanning a whole line as in 10, is of rhythmic rather than semantic import (as far as the two can be separated). This elemental rhythm "present in the nursery bedroom" (11) pervades the seasons of the household— "April," "autumn," "winter"—and perhaps its ages, if the members of the "evening circle" of the last line reasonably exclude one of nursery status. We remember that April was "the cruellest month" in *The Waste Land*[2] Its ailanthus, something of an exotic and particularly beautiful with its delicately tinted leaf buds opening, is described as rank in the double sense of lushly growing and of disagreeable odor. We may perhaps see personal association behind the choice of a tree hardly common in the Mississippi valley, but its conjectural presence in the Eliots' front yard does not consign it to the class of "private symbol" nor impair its cogency as image here. (The ailanthus is the Chinese "tree of heaven"—so called because of its upward-turning branches and twigs—a circumstance possibly rewarding to the seeker of irony.) The concreteness of this scene as of the still life in the next line and the domestic interior of the one following compels our recognition of the "life force" beneath the social veneer much as "Hypocrite lecteur" drew acknowledgement of shared experience. The "low" diction exemplified by "dooryard" (a deliberate Americanism?) and "gaslight" has the same bearing, as has also the olfactory imagery in connection with objects whose color and form might otherwise be signalized. Whether "circle" can be read without ulterior connotation depends perhaps upon the completeness of reader identification with the simple home scene.

The rest of section I follows the new direction set by the pivotal line 15, but its alleged outwardness is after all only a necessary attention to what impinges upon the area of our interests. The fauna and flotsam touch "our curiosity" or typify "our losses."

15   The river is within us, the sea is all about us;
16 The sea is the land's edge, also, the granite
17 Into which it reaches, the beaches where it tosses
18 Its hints of earlier and other creation:
19 The starfish, the hermit crab, the whale's backbone;
20 The pools where it offers to our curiosity
21 The more delicate algae and the sea anemone.
22 It tosses up our losses, the torn seine,
23 The shattered lobsterpot, the broken oar
24 And the gear of foreign dead men.

The rhythm is closer and more pronouncedly four-stressed. The structural principle here seems to be a coral-like branching in which the skeletal outline is clearly discernible. Thus, 15 gives us "The river...the sea...;" in 16 and 17 "sea" equals "land's edge," then "granite" plus relative clause and "beaches" plus relative clause; the object in the second clause, the "hints" of 18, develop into the three members of 19 (among these "hermit crab," Eliot informs us[3] is an inadvertency); "pools" (20) appears to be another offshoot from the "sea" branch—it has a two-line clause modifier but is not further subdivided. The separate second sentence is still about the sea, but under its less gentle aspect. In these catalogues we may find an enumeration of objects which fascinated a small boy during a New England summer, and we recall that this season was skipped in the riverside year above. (This is not to press for an autobiographical reading, but to suggest a new thread of coherence, for on whose experience can a poet better draw than on his own?)

Internal rhyme where it occurs is at close range: "ever, however" (7), "*land's...granite*" (16), "reaches, the beaches" (17) (the same combination as in "Words, after speech, reach" [*BN* 142]), "tosses up our losses" (22). There are sound links like the recurring vowel of "all" (15), "also" (16), "tosses" (17), "more" (21), "tosses," "losses," "torn" (22), "oar" (23), and the half-rhyme series "*earlier*" (18), "st*a*rfish," "h*e*rmit" (19), "where," "our" (20), "more" (21), "our," "torn" (22), "oar" (23) "gear," "*foreign*" (24). These, however significant musically, are structurally of less import than the syntactic-semantic correspondences of phrase groups such as "within us"—"about us" (15), "torn seine"—"shattered lobsterpot"— "broken oar" (22-23). Sound values are so far subordinate, but in the rest of section I they loom large indeed, where the "many voices" of the changeful ocean shape sound and rhythm and line length.

```
24              The sea has many voices,
25  Many gods and many voices.
26              The salt is on the briar rose,
27  The fog is in the fir trees.
28              The sea howl
29  And the sea yelp, are different voices
30  Often together heard; the whine in the rigging,
31  The menace and caress of wave that breaks on
    water,
32  The distant rote in the granite teeth,
33  And  the wailing warning from the approaching
    headland
34  Are all sea voices, and the heaving groaner
35  Rounded homewards, and the seagull:
36  And under the oppression of the silent fog
37  The tolling bell
38  Measures time not our time, rung by the unhurried
39  Ground swell, a time
40  Older than the time of chronometers, older
41  Than time counted by anxious worried women
42  Lying awake, calculating the future,
```

43 Trying to unweave, unwind, unravel
44 And piece together the past and the future,
45 Between midnight and dawn, when the past is all
    deception,
46 The future futureless, before the morning watch
47 When time stops and time is never ending;
48 And the ground swell, that is and was from the
    beginning,
49 Clangs
50 The bell.

The suggestion of stichomythia after 24 middle introduces a dramatic note whose strongest reminiscence is of
Murder in the Cathedral.[4] The effect is considerably muted, but
surely the "anxious worried women" are sisters to the chorus
at Canterbury who "smelt them, the death-bringers" and
whose animal memories and lobster and crab and sea
anemone emerged from a far more sinister context than *The
Dry Salvages* I. Briar rose and fir tree replace rose garden and
box circle of *Burnt Norton*, where, as in Thomas' answer to the
women of Canterbury, "Human kind cannot bear very much
reality." This economy of self-allusiveness is perhaps the
most successful of Eliot's inbreeding experiments.

The "sea howl / And the sea yelp" (28-29) and "the whine
in the rigging" (30) bear out the implicit animal imagery. The
word order of "Often together heard" (30) gives us pause.
Why is the regular alternation of stressed and unstressed
syllables afforded by a more normal "often heard together"
so pointedly avoided? The rhythm is in effect sprung, but its
most interesting feature is the numerical diminuendo of
three syllables, two, one, whose temporal value is in inverse
ratio, making the three units equivalent as it were in their
moments of leverage. In "menace and caress" (31) the
balanced contrast is perfect, the two nouns being exactly
opposite in meaning, stress and vowel arrangement.
"Wave...on water" (31) begins the appropriately recurring
w-alliteration that is picked up in "wailing warning" (33),
"worried women / ...awake" (41-42), "unweave, unwind"
(43). The halves of 32 are parallel, with "in" as a kind of
extra-metrical connective; the reversed order of the vowels
in the disyllabic adjectives make for variety and sense of

pattern—at least to the eye, the second vowel in each word being mute or nearly so. The subdued metaphor in "granite teeth" and the peculiar sense of motion conveyed by "the approaching headland" (33) increase the voices' vividness. Of their variety there can be no doubt when we add to wind and "wave that breaks on water" and surf on shore and foghorn, the rounding or murmuring of the groaner Eliot glosses for us as a whistling buoy, together with the seagull's cry. But richest of all in symbolic possibilities and power of evocation is the bell buoy tolled by no man but by the ceaseless ground swell with its primeval force and rhythm older even than the river god. Time and what transcends it, and the hours it leaves untouched, and the tangled interplay of past and future once more demand attention. But the timelessness of these lines is not that of the intense and inward moment— rather has it an impersonally eternal quality and a tone with which the Krishna reference of the third section will harmonize without adjustment. The short lines and the frank onomatopoeia and the interweaving of earlier themes (time past and time future, end and beginning) lend this section an effectiveness that is not without virtuosity.

Section II falls into two parts nearly equal in length. The first is a variety of sestina whose inter-stanzaic rhymes, mostly on two or three syllables, are by their very remoteness from each other impressive less as a mere *tour de force* than as an ably sustained echo series evincing a truly remarkable command of language. The careful inexactness of the matching words in several instances effectively prevents any suggestion of *Practical Cats* which the double and triple rhymes usually characteristic of nonsense verse might convey. The meter, of course (the favorite free four-stress), is an important factor in the creation of tone which the phrasal handling (especially of the "end" motif) admirably subserves. Examination in isolation of the rhyme sequence reveals a vacillating relationship among the end words of lines 3, 4 and 5 of each stanza while lines 1, 2 and 6 in each maintain a consistent resemblance. The identity of the end words in the first and sixth stanzas serves to resolve previous discrepancies and to close the unit.

(1st lines)	wailing-trailing-failing-sailing-bailing-wailing
(2nd lines)	flowers-hours-powers-cowers-lowers-flowers
(3rd lines)	motionless-emotionless-devotionless-oceanless-erosionless-motionless
(4th lines)	wreckage-breakage-leakage-wastage-dockage-wreckage
(5th lines)	unprayable-reliable-undeniable-liable-unprayable-prayable
(6th lines)	annunciation-renunciation-annunciation-destination-examination-Annunciation

Syntactically the first stanza forms a compound question, rephrased in more specifically human terms in the first two lines of the fourth. The answer, dealing with the interminability rather than the eternity of the phenomena under consideration, is divided into proportionate line groups, the first comprising stanzas two and three and the second the last four lines of the fourth stanza together with the fifth; the sixth stanza recapitulates while it concludes the restless questioning.

Among the most evident features of the diction throughout this stanzaic passage are the prevalence of *-ing* words, both participles and gerunds, and a marked tendency toward reduplication of stressed words.[5] We have the feeling, without a single occurrence of the actual tense form, of the present progressive, and a *legato* effect as of tied notes in music which do not so much retard as insist upon the continuity of the melodic flow.

51 Where is there an end of it, the soundless wailing,
52 The silent withering of autumn flowers
53 Dropping their petals and remaining motionless;
54 Where is there an end to the drifting wreckage,
55 The prayer of the bone on the beach, the unprayable
56 Prayer at the calamitous annunciation?

Muteness—"soundless," "silent," "unprayable"—decay—"withering," "autumn," "Dropping," "wreckage"—and inertia—"remaining motionless," "drifting"—are the somewhat gloomy components of the opening stanza of the group. The "annunciation" with which the question closes, while it anticipates the capitalized "one Annunciation" at the end of the sixth stanza, is here only "calamitous"—*calamitosus* can mean "liable to be injured by storms"—and seems to prognosticate a *dies irae* from which there is no appeal. Flower and bone, both lifeless now, are fitting symbols. We look for revealing relationship, and amid the welter of sea-voices are struck by the unuttered cry of human pain, the unspoken grief of wakeful women, fishermen's wives many times bereaved perhaps before their loss is actual. One hesitates to equate outright the "soundless wailing" and "withering... autumn flowers" with the women of section I and their mute lament, but the analogy is there, and the breath of fatalism detected in the stanza accords better with the dramatic attitude such a *persona* legitimately gives scope for than with the poet's own position as established earlier in the *Quartets*. The "drifting wreckage" clearly includes the "losses" of lines 22-24, and the "bone on the beach" may be that of whale or whaleman. The twice repeated "Where is there an end" (besides contributing to the uncommon initial rhyme series, "Where"-"Where"-"Prayer"-"There" [51, 54, 56, 57]) both serves as refrain and sets the rhetorical tone that keeps the whole an open question.

57　⁶There is no end, but addition: the trailing
58　Consequence of further days and hours,
59　While emotion takes to itself the emotionless
60　Years of living among the breakage
61　Of what was believed in as the most reliable—
62　And therefore the fittest for renunciation.

The tentative answer offers no surcease, but more of the same. "Consequence" would appear to be rather "sequence" intensified than "result." Time is very much with us in "days and hours," "Years." The precise extension of "emotion" is difficult to determine, but its psychological meaning is surely only part of the comples. Whatever the scale of the agitation it indicates, it seems to attract into the microcosmic vortex the apathetic temporal drifting among the shattered idols or ideals of a life upon which "renunciation" is forced by circumstance, a negative purification indeed.

63   There is the final addition, the failing
64   Pride or resentment at failing powers,
65   The unattached devotion which might pass for
       devotionless,
66   In a drifting boat with a slow leakage,
67   The silent listening to the undeniable
68   Clamour of the bell of the last annunciation.

The "final addition" of approaching death is, significantly, not seen as an "end." Detachment masks as indifference. There is receptivity in the "silent listening;" the clamorous summons seen first as "calamitous," then as inevitable, is now not unwelcome. We have climbed to some awareness of the transcendent and positive role of suffering.

69   Where is the end of them, the fishermen sailing
70   Into the wind's tail, where the fog cowers?
71   We cannot think of a time that is oceanless
72   Or of an ocean not littered with wastage
73   Or of a future that is not liable
74   Like the past, to have no destination.

This fourth stanza expresses more concretely the problem of individual destinies. The implicit imagery of line 70 adds to the vividness, as does the sound play of 69-70 to the rhythmic current and rhetorical effectiveness. The pairing is at some distance-"sailing"-"tail," "fishermen"-"wind's," "fishermen"-"fog." Nasals and short *i*'s (by no means restricted to the *-ing* forms) which are present in fairly high concentration throughout the sestina are here perhaps the more evident for their proximity to other linking devices.

The things "we cannot think of" seem at first a strange mixture, but the medley resolves itself into the familiar concern with time and its relations. After an almost frivolous passing from the timeles ocean of section I to oceanless time in line 71, with the waste-littered ocean of 72 we come into a confused mingling of echoes of the "waste sad time" (*BN* 177), "Men and bits of paper" (*BN* 107) and the drifted wreckage of the first stanza of the second section. The negatives in 71, 73-74 need unraveling. "We cannot think . . . of a future that is not liable . . . to have no destination" can be stripped down to "the future is threatened with goallessness." The meaning of "end" now broadens beyond mere "terminus." 74 speaks of the failure of the past in predicting that of the future. Long ago (*BN* 3) we read of "time future contained in time past." Their eventual fusion renders single the problem of time, be it of perpetuity or purpose.

75   We have to think of them as forever bailing,
76   Setting and hauling, while the North East lowers
77   Over shallow banks unchanging and erosionless
78   Or drawing their money, drying sails at dockage;
79   Not as making a trip that will be unpayable
80   For a haul that will not bear examination.

The same illusion of perpetual motion haunts the fifth stanza. The epithets in line 77 are strikingly confirmed by Rachel Carson in *The Sea Around Us*.[7] Why, in 79-80, does the poet dismiss the thought of unprosperous voyages? Perhaps the eschatological undertone detectable in the final reckoning for good (78) or ill (79-80) is intended as covert reference to the hinted redemption to come through the "one Annunciation" of the final stanza.

81   There is no end of it, the voiceless wailing,
82   No end to the withering of withered flowers,
83   To the movement of pain that is painless and motionless,
84   To the drift of the sea and the drifting wreckage,
85   The bone's prayer to Death its God. Only the hardly, barely prayable
86   Prayer of the one Annunciation.

The end denied is that of the quasi-infinite process of passive purification. "The bone's prayer" in 85 seems to be one more object of "to," three times expressed above. The shift from "unprayable" (55) to "barely prayable" (85) accompanies the altered connotation of "Annunciation" to its frankly Incarnational value at the end of the sestina. "Only" in 85 could have the force of "but," making the sense of the whole "there is no end to human misery save in the concept of [it would be too much to say "in its acceptance as"] Christian sacrifice." "Death its God," at first strongly redolent of Frazer, then undergoes a transmutation, but the triumph is not yet explicit.

The peculiarly compelling rhythm of these rhymed lines, a real sea rhythm in some, arises from the widely varied placing of stresses and counting of slacks—almost no two lines are alike in this respect (the exceptions are those closest to the basic dactyllic pattern: / ˘ ˘ / ˘ ˘ / ˘ ˘ / ˘, viz., 57, 63, 72)—and from the lines' all ending on unstressed syllables (considering "hours" [58] as disyllabic to match "flowers," "powers," etc.). The one "swollen" line, 85, makes a fitting *rallentando* before the close of the stanzaic interlude.

The second half of section II corresponds structurally and tonally with unrhymed passages which in *Burnt Norton* II and *East Coker* II also follow the brief incursions into rhyming forms. Syntactically compact, the "prose diction" of the next lines falls into a rhetoric of its own.

> 87   It seems, as one becomes older,
> 88   That the past has another pattern, and ceases to be
>   a mere sequence—
> 89   Or even development: the latter a partial fallacy,
> 90   Encouraged by superficial notions of evolution,
> 91   Which becomes, in the popular mind, a means of
>   disowning the past.

In the changing perspective of advancing years relationships realign themselves. The denial of sequence points to a grasp of the simultaneity of past experience. The glimpse of "another pattern" is a further acknowledgement of the liberating pattern of *Burnt Norton* V which conduced to "stillness." The continual blending and interchange in the *Quartets* of the notions of time and movement, or of movement in time and space, has already united presentness with stillness at "the still point" central to awareness of the transient and giving coherence to what is otherwise discrete or discordant, and on a level deeper than that habitual to "the popular mind."

> 92   The moments of happiness—not the sense of well-
>   being,
> 93   Fruition, fulfilment, security or affection,
> 94   Or even a very good dinner, but the sudden
>   illumination—
> 95   We had the experience but missed the meaning,

96 And approach to the meaning restores the experience
97 In a different form, beyond any meaning
98 We can assign to happiness.

The careful sifting of occasions, largely extrinsic, of
feeling happiness leaves in its purity the "sudden illumination" which is the possession (however fleeting) of happiness,
imparted like the breathings of the Spirit and like these
sometimes resisted, sometimes meeting in the unprepared a
limited but genuine welcome. Those who "had the experience
but missed the meaning" in *The Family Reunion*[8] tried by
mutual confrontation to "approach...the meaning" and so to
"restore the experience." That this is possible the poet avers
in 96-98, while admitting a qualitative difference that
represents if not an intensification at least a broadening of
subjective appreciation (a matter of individual capacity), or a
clearing of irrelevancies that might have clouded the original
experience, or a poet's relaying of the same. The insistent
"meaning" of 95, 96 and 97 (and 99) suggests more strongly
than would an attempted definition where to focus our
attention. So does the aposiopesis of 92.

98   I have said before
99 That the past experience revived in the meaning
100 Is not the experience of one life only
101 But of many generations—not forgetting
102 Something that is probably quite ineffable:
103 The backward look behind the assurance
104 Of recorded history, the backward half-look
105 Over the shoulder, towards the primitive terror.

The nature of the experience was indicated in *East Coker*
194ff.[9]—"a lifetime burning in every moment / And not the
lifetime of one man only"—and here we are bidden look
behind even the "old stones" to the unpropitiated river god
of the first section.

104-105 sketch in the fewest possible strokes one of the
memorable images of the poem. The economy of the drawing
contrasts with the deliberately wordy "Something that is
probably quite ineffable" with which it is prefaced. "I have
said before" (98) like "I shall say it again" (*EC* 136) becomes a

rhetorical formula introducing a more or less hieratic pronouncement.

106 Now, we come to discover that the moments of agony
107 (Whether, or not, due to misunderstanding,
108 Having hoped for the wrong things or dreaded the wrong things,
109 Is not in question) are likewise permanent
110 With such permanence as time has. We appreciate this better
111 In the agony of others, nearly experienced,
112 Involving ourselves, than in our own.
113 For our own past is covered by the currents of action,
114 But the torment of others remains an experience
115 Unqualified, unworn by subsequent attrition.
116 People change, and smile: but the agony abides.

"Moments of agony" represent the obverse of "moments of happiness" (92). (The cause-disclaiming parenthesis does not disqualify *East Coker* 124-128[10] with its abnegations.) Their "permanence," hardly a quality expected of "moments," comes as a discovery and is allied to the enduringness, first as felt, then as understood, of the other moments of "sudden illumination." In neither instance is it uninterruptedness of state that is claimed, but a certain solidarity of human experience, vertical in the history of the race and horizontal in the range of social sympathies. In speaking of the suffering moments the emphasis is far less on the purely personal plane which predominates in the earlier references to intensely realized—and desirable—experience here recognized as happiness. All this is readily explicable in the light of the doctrine of the Mystical Body of Christ, it it be not premature (at this stage of the poem) to press so downright an interpretation. "Such permanence as time has" may be found where, in these moments, it impinges upon eternity, at its intersection with the timeless. The observations of 110-115 need no comment but the reader's tacit testimony to their justice, a valid test of universality. The character of the words "currents" (113) and "unworn" (115) retains the spirit of the tidal imagery to which we return again and again in *The Dry Salvages.*

117 Time the destroyer is time the preserver,
118 Like the river with its cargo of dead Negroes, cows
 and chicken coops,
119 The bitter apple and the bite in the apple.
120 And the ragged rock in the restless waters,
121 Waves wash over it, fogs conceal it;
122 On a halcyon day it is merely a monument,
123 In navigable weather it is always a seamark
124 To lay a course by: but in the sombre season
125 Or the sudden fury, is what it always was.

The clue to the paradox is in the river reference. This not at all trite river of time is, as in lines 7-8, "destroyer, reminder / Of what men choose to forget." 118 may depict aftermath of flood, or oddly assorted and grimly associated freight of morgue and market. The *memento mori* is reenforced by the symbol of the Fall in the apple of line 119, which as objective fact ("The bitter apple") and subjective effect ("the bite in the apple") seems (syntactically, too) as much bound up with time as it is independent verbless musing. It probably belongs not with cows and chicken coops but parallel with river as object of "like" (118).

We leave the river for the sea with the transitional and syntactically loose alliterative line 120 whose prominence in point of sound pattern places it at the crest of a series of ascending frequency—"covered by currents" (113), "unqualified, unworn" (115), "attrition...agony abides" (115-116), "Time...time" (117), "cargo...cows...coops" (118), "bitter apple...bite...apple" (119), while after "ragged rock... restless" and "waters, / Waves wash" (120-121) the pace slows to "conceal...halcyon" (121-122), "merely a monument" (122), "seamark" (123)—"sombre season" (124)—"sudden" (125). The *s* sounds form an interesting supplementary pattern, with softer sibilants in the ascendancy from "restless" (120) to the initials of "sombre season," while the last lines of the passage grow heavy with *z* values for the final *s* of "always" (twice), "is" and "was" and the medial *s* of "season."

The six lines devoted to the rock tempt us to allegorize its role and its weathers. The *Choruses from "The Rock"* (which in *CPP* immediately precede *Four Quartets*) contain in crude or inchoate form much that is more subtly and effectively conveyed in the *Quartets*. If we hear the voice of the churchman, though, in this passage of *The Dry Salvages*, we do not lose sight of the rock as feature of the New England seacoast, while its possibilities as symbol are further enriched. "What it always was" is suitably left undefined, and the direct presentation of its successive faces has a telling objectivity that metaphor would only weaken.

Section III opens and closes with a reminiscence from the *Bhagavadgita* of Krishna's answer to Arjuna's dilemma as a warrior committed to action and attracted to contemplation. Eliot's "do not think of the fruit of action" (163), properly understood, crystallizes with thematic adequacy an important issue of the section.

The first two lines are a bevy of small and colorless words such as habitually relieve the intenser passages.

126 I sometimes wonder if that is what Krishna meant—
127 Among other things—or one way of putting the same thing:

The contrast is at once apparent in the continued time-speculation which in 128-130 employs concrete symbols which are described in words suggesting colors—"Rose," "lavender," "yellow" (actually the only true adjective of color here), even "faded."

128 That the future is a faded song, a Royal Rose or a lavender spray
129 Of wistful regret for those who are not yet here to regret,
130 Pressed between yellow leaves of a book that has never been opened.

Again, then, we find "time future contained in time past" (*BN* 3). The gentle insistence of "regret"-"yet"-"regret" and the carrying of the same vowel into "Pressed"-"yellow"-"never" impose a certain restraint on the paradox already muffled in consonants (far in the majority, while many of the vowels are silent or weak) in easily enunciated order. Another sequence, to whose force the line position of the words contribute, is:

```
128 future
129                  not yet
130                             never
```

"Wistful" is well placed (near the beginning of the middle line of the three) to set the tone.

Line 131, "And the way up is the way down, the way forward is the way back," takes us back to the epigraph, and makes the further fusion the context renders appropriate: "forward" and "back" are other ways of saying (cf. 127) "future" and "past."

132 You cannot face it steadily, but this thing is sure,
133 That time is no healer: the patient is no longer here.

What is not faced steadily is known in separate "moments of agony," which, because of their "permanence" (see 109-110) time does not heal. The patient who "is no longer here," like the train passengers who "are not the same people who left that station" (141) and the ocean voyagers who "are not those who saw the harbour / Receding" (152-153), has suffered a sea change of sorts, and we look to the "wounded surgeon" of *East Coker* IV on the one hand, and "Phlebas the Phoenician" of *The Waste Land* IV[11] on the other for commentary on the enigma of pain and its operation in the human spirit.

134 When the train starts and the passengers are settled
135 To fruit, periodicals and business letters
136 (And those who saw them off have left the platform)
137 Their faces relax from grief into relief,
138 To the sleepy rhythm of a hundred hours.
139 Fare forward, travellers! not escaping from the past
140 Into different lives, or into any future;
141 You are not the same people who left that station
142 Or who will arrive at any terminus,
143 While the narrowing rails slide together behind you;
144 And on the deck of the drumming liner
145 Watching the furrow that widens behind you,
146 You shall not think "the past is finished"
147 Or "the future is before us."
148 At nightfall, in the rigging and the aerial,

149 Is a voice descanting (though not to the ear,
150 The murmuring shell of time, and not in any
    language)
151 "Fare forward, you who think that you are
    voyaging;
152 You are not those who saw the harbour
153 Receding, or those who will disembark.

The details from the realistic railroad scene to the mystic
sea voice add up to a total impression of mutability
triumphed over by the acceptance of change. The false
solution of escape detected and depicted in 134-140 is not
very unlike the vacancy of the underground riders of *Burnt
Norton* III and *East Coker* III; the faces in all three *Quartets* are
particular objects of scrutiny. An interesting doubling of
syntax occurs in 143, which line properly belongs with the
two preceding although its precise adverbial relationship
would be hard to define in terms of tense logic—past "left,"
future "will arrive" and present "slide" blend only in the
transcendent grasp of the rare moments. At the same time
"the narrowing rails" offer a nice rhetorical balance of "the
furrow that widens" (145), and to both apply equally the
cautions of 146-147. The perfection of the metaphor for
"ear," the "murmuring shell of time," dawns on us with a
realization of the rarity of the device so simply resorted to
here. The "Fare forward" message is near refrain in the lines
which follow.

154 Here between the hither and the farther shore
155 While time is withdrawn, consider the future
156 And the past with an equal mind.
157 At the moment which is not of action or inaction
158 You can receive this: 'on whatever sphere of being
159 The mind of a man may be intent
160 At the time of death'—that is the one action
161 (And the time of death is every moment)
162 Which shall fructify in the lives of others:
163 And do not think of the fruit of action.
164 Fare forward.

The brief participation in the absolute, "While time is
withdrawn," invites a weighing of values *aequo animo*, remote

from the eddying of passions, before proceeding farther or being drawn into the whirlpool that swallowed Phlebas. This detached moment represents optimum receptivity of the offered wisdom. From the syntax it would seem that being intent on a given sphere of being is an "action." Regarded as a more or less high degree of contemplation or (Christian mystical) union the sphere attained may well be a source of benefit to other members of the race and "fructify in the lives of others." The parenthetical line 161 is less paradox than reminder of what many men "choose to forget," and of the successive deaths that are part of all organic changes and therefore of all vital experience (in the natural order, and, by analogy, in the supernatural)—at every step, Eliot has shown us, there is something to relinquish, but the emptying is not an end in itself: "the darkness shall be the light, and the stillness the dancing" (*EC* 129).

Life as a voyage is not an arresting image, but its eminent naturalness prevents it from being trite while it serves as quiet background to the kaleidoscopic play of symbols, begun it is true before any voyage reference in the "faded song," "Royal Rose" and "lavender spray" of line 128—these would seem to have been chosen for their general pastness (there are no other songs or lavender in the *Quartets*, and while "Royal Rose" looks forward to *Little Gidding* with its "broken king" and "spectre of a Rose" [LG 27 and 186] it is emblematic rather of English monarchy than of a Stuart sovereign and recalls ancient faction more than seventeenth century party strife).

165   O voyagers, O seamen,
166 You who come to port, and you whose bodies
167 Will suffer the trial and judgement of the sea,
168 Or whatever event, this is your real destination."
169 So Krishna, as when he admonished Arjuna
170 On the field of battle.
171   Not fare well,
172 But fare forward, voyagers.

We observe that it is only the bodies of the mariners that the sea exercises jurisdiction over, or that suffer "whatever event." The spiritual goal, the "real destination," is not to be confounded with their material fate. The exact nature, however, of the "real destination" must be deduced from the foregoing negations. We must remember the "fare forward...not escaping" (139) when inclined to equate this passivity with Nirvana. The final emphases of section III, "field of battle," "Not fare well," "fare forward," are not an invitation to inaction.

The brief section IV with its three sentence-stanzas might be called a liturgical lyric, echoing as it does the "Bidding Prayer" of the *Book of Common Prayer* whose flexible clauses are introduced by an ever so slightly varying formula like "Ye shall pray for... [12]

173 Lady, whose shrine stands on the promontory,
174 Pray for all those who are in ships, those
175 Whose business has to do with fish, and
176 Those concerned with every lawful traffic
177 And those who conduct them.

178   [13]Repeat a prayer also on behalf of
179 Women who have seen their sons or husbands
180 Setting forth, and not returning:
181 Figlia del tuo figlio,
182 Queen of heaven.

183   Also pray for those who were in ships, and
184 Ended their voyage on the sand, in the sea's lips
185 Or in the dark throat which will not reject them
186 Or wherever cannot reach them the sound of the
        sea bell's
187 Perpetual angelus.

The triple prayer to Our Lady proceeds with nice balance and variation to beg her intercession for those "who are in ships" and those "who were in ships" and the anxious worried women whose fears were justified. The invocations come at the beginning of the first stanza and, doubly, at the end of the second where they may do duty also for the third which is without apostrophe. The phrasing of the petitions runs from the legal-sounding enumeration of the first through the simple understatement of the second to the figured series of the third, considerable rhetorical contrast for so short a space and within a "pray for" pattern that is substantially the same in each.

The line organization appears loose and intentionally irregular—rhythmic tensions are at a minimum and stresses on the whole hard to apportion with certainty. Sense units are carried over line-ends in a way that is especially conspicuous in 174, 175 and 183 where the comma marking the syntactical pause occurs just one word before the end, and in 178 where the object of "on behalf of" is deferred until the next line. The lines with two exceptions end with unstressed words or syllables, while "bell's" (186) has surely only secondary stress as "lips" (184) probably has.

The sound components of the individual stanzas suit their differences in diction. The first is predominantly consonantal. Most frequent here are the *z*-sounding *s*, and the fricatives represented by *sh* and *th*: "who*s*e" (twice), "tho*s*e" (four times), "bu*s*iness," "ha*s*;" "*sh*rine," "*sh*ips," "fi*sh*;" "*th*e," "*th*ose," "wi*th*" (twice), "*th*em." The vowels run to the less colorful values of *o* (seventeen occurrences in five lines) and unobtrusive short *i* sounds and their near equivalents: "in ships," "business," "with fish," "with . . . traffic," and probably the final *y* in "Lady," "promontory" and "every." The second stanza offers longer vowels, especially that of "Rep*ea*t," "s*ee*n," "Figlia," "figlio," "Qu*ee*n," and the voiceless *s* and *f* series: "al*s*o," "*s*een," "*s*ons," "*s*etting;" "behal*f*," "*f*orth," "Figlia," "figlio." The Italian line (*Paradiso* xxxiii, 1) with its liquids and vowel combinations brings in a note of reverent tenderness suited to its sense and context. The third stanza is the most variegated as well as the most adorned. "The sand," "the sea's lips" and "the dark throat" show vowel colors ranging from bright through pale to dark even as their local accessibility outstrips the watcher's vision. There is consonant chime in "sand" and "sound," rhyme in "ships" and "lips," echo in "will not reject them"-"cannot reach them," "in the sea's lips"-"the sea bell's" (even the placing of the *'s* in the last pair is artistically significant), and the rhythmic sweep of "the sound of the sea bell's/Perpetual angelus" amply justifies the peculiar inversion in line 186. The rhythmic scheme is generally clearer in this last stanza where genuine dactyls and indisputable spondees give a classical ring.

The fifth section, typographically unbroken, falls into two rhythmic units, lines 188-219 which read like dramatic blank verse in which a pentameter pattern is superimposed upon the natural four-stress movement, and lines 220-237 which are clearly three-stressed. The first long sentence is a kind of catalogue of superstitious fads.

188 To communicate with Mars, converse with spirits,
189 To report the behaviour of the sea monster,
190 Describe the horoscope, haruspicate or scry,
191 Observe disease in signatures, evoke
192 Biography from the wrinkles of the palm
193 And tragedy from fingers; release omens
194 By sortilege, or tea leaves, riddle the inevitable
195 With playing cards, fiddle with pentagrams
196 Or barbituric acids, or dissect
197 The recurrent image into pre-conscious terrors—
198 To explore the womb, or tomb, or dreams; all these
    are usual
199 Pastimes and drugs, and features of the press:
200 And always will be, some of them especially
201 When there is distress of nations and perplexity
202 Whether on the shores of Asia, or in the Edgware
    Road.

The arsenal of verbs in the initial infinitive series is impressive for its thesaurus-like proportions: "communicate," "converse," "report," "Describe," "haruspicate," "scry," "Observe," "evoke," "release," "riddle," "fiddle," "dissect," "explore." Of the thirteen verbs in the first eleven lines eight are transitive in function, and seven of these take their objects without so much as an intervening adjective (and of these three dispense even with the definite article). The only adjectives that are purely descriptive and not really part of the noun they modify (like "playing cards" and "barbituric acids") are "recurrent," "pre-conscious" and "usual" (197), and each of these has somehow to do with time. The massed nouns, none of which is neutral in this charged context, accumulate more and more of Eliot's somewhat weary contempt[14] for the soothsayer's stock in trade, and in general for all "charms, omens, dreams and such like fooleries." These poor gropings are seen as at least ineffectual if not actually blaspheming against the future.

203 Men's curiosity searches past and future

204 And clings to that dimension. But to apprehend
205 The point of intersection of the timeless
206 With time, is an occupation for the saint—
207 No occupation either, but something given
208 And taken, in a lifetime's death in love,
209 Ardour and selflessness and self-surrender.

Here again is "love...and self-surrender," a specifically Christian version of the disposition requisite for the apprehension broached at the successive high points of the poem. (An index of Eliot's impact on contemporary thought and phraseology is the appearance without quotes of the expression "the point of intersection of the timeless with time" in an article[15] by Anne Fremantle in which she says that the Church dwells there.)

210 For most of us, there is only the unattended
211 Moment, the moment in and out of time,
212 The distraction fit, lost in a shaft of sunlight,
213 The wild thyme unseen, or the winter lightning
214 Or the waterfall, or music heard so deeply
215 That it is not heard at all, but you are the music
216 While the music lasts.

And here again is the gathering of images from the earlier *Quartets* (cf. *BN* 172, "Sudden in a shaft of sunlight;" *BN* 147, "the stillness of the violin, while the note lasts;" *EC* 130-131, "Whisper of running streams, and winter lightning. / The wild thyme unseen...."). To identify "you" in 215 (after all, part of the first person plural) we go best to "My words echo / Thus, in your mind" (*BN* 14-15). That we are not yet (in the "For most of us" sentence) dealing with supernatural persons or experiences is clear from the next lines:

216   These are only hints and guesses,
217 Hints followed by guesses; and the rest
218 Is prayer, observance, discipline, thought and action.
219 The hint half guessed, the gift half understood, is Incarnation.

(This is to read "hint" [219] as metonymy [or ellipsis] for "that which is hinted at.") This is the crux of he poem prepared for by antecedent grappling with facts that point to and are in turn illuminated by the one tremendous fact, and foreshadowed in the positive experiences ordered in its light. The besetting problems of time and relation here find perfect reconciliation. In the cogent phrasing of a modern theologian, "the action in time and place of an Eternal Being has two aspects: there is the completed action in time and place and there is the eternal act of the Eternal Being beyond time and place and outside time and place. Because the action is in time, it happened at one time and in one place; because it was the act of an Eternal Being it happens at all times and in all places."[16] Accordingly, the "timeless has come into time, the invisible has become seen, the intangible palpable, God has become man."[17] The only valid aspiration to transcend time is then through the Incarnation: "We are made mystically one with the human nature of Christ, and therefore we participate in some manner in the eternal character of the actions of Christ."[18]

With this in mind the rest is clear:

220 Here the impossible union[19]
221 Of spheres of existence is actual,
222 Here the past and future
223 Are conquered, and reconciled,
224 Where action were otherwise movement
225 Of that which is only moved
226 And has in it no source of movement—
227 Driven by demonic, chthonic
228 Powers. And right action is freedom
229 From past and future also.

Krishna's answer is not falsified but completed with the fullness of truth. Phrase for phrase ("spheres of being"—or of existence, "the future and the past," "action . . .") its points are lifted into the new harmony—where there was "neither" now is "both"—"the impossible union . . . is actual." Deprivation is conquest, purgation approaches union, the "real destination" is the imperfectly realized but devoutly sought goal of redeemed mankind, union with God. The earlier association of "the farther shore" (154) and "the time of death" (160) recalls the restless spirits, unburied and unredeemed, evoked as long ago as *BN* III,[20] whose action had "in it no source of movement" (226) but who were literally "Driven by...chthonic/Powers" (227-228). These, like the living dead of *The Waste Land*, have no part in what is partly the fruit of "prayer, observance, discipline, thought and action" (218) and partly "gift half understood" (219).

```
230  For most of us, this is the aim
231  Never here to be realised;
232  Who are only undefeated
233  Because we have gone on trying;
234  We, content at the last
235  If our temporal reversion nourish
236  (Not too far from the yew-tree)
237  The life of significant soil.
```

In terms of present attainment and recognized limitations, "most of us" can at best hope for occasional "moment[s] in and out of time" (211) which like actual graces raise the fainting spirit to "go on trying." Our capitulation to time is itself a victory, death nourishing life, time past containing time future, where the yew-tree keeps us mindful of our immortality. The return here is to the first section of *East Coker* and the dancers "under earth/Nourishing the corn" (*EC* 39-40). Their lives had exemplified the natural, good but with emphasis on its physical and material aspects. We who follow them to the grave have more than glimpsed our higher destiny, and in the supernatural order restored by the Incarnation and accessible to us in proportion to our response to grace the "significant soil" betokens resurrection as the "meaning" missed in former interpersonal experience becomes genuinely sacramental.

There are no syntactical problems in this section if "We, content..." (234) be accepted as a nominative absolute. Throughout we find repetitive appositions or paratactic series ("the unattended/Moment, the moment..." [210-211], "hints and guesses,/Hints followed by guesses" [216-217], "the hint half guessed, the gift half understood" [219], and verbal reduplications ("timeless/With time" [205-206], "selflessness and self-surrender" [209], "music" three times [214-216], "movement"—"moved"-"movement" [224-226]) whose role is chiefly rhetorical. A tension between contradictories, not quite the same as in Krishna's speech, is variously voiced in "an occupation"-"No occupation" (206-

207), "lifetime's death" (208), "in and out of time" 211), "heard"-"not heard" (214-215), "impossible"-"actual" (220-221). Possibly included here would be "Asia" (the exotic) and "Edgware Road" (the commonplace) (202). There are close internal rhymes—"riddle"-"fiddle" (194-195), "womb, or tomb" (198), "daemonic, chthonic" (227)—but few other conspicuous sound links. The diction is richly associative, especially within the frame of the *Quartets*, but for the most part not unusually complex—"unattended" (210) offers the reading "not waited for," "unexpected," along with "unaccompanied;" "our temporal reversion" has a legal twist and a physical root meaning. The punctuation is orthodox with the exception of the colon at the end of 199. This, in keeping with Eliot's occasional prose usage, seems to be employed simply to indicate a longer pause than a semi-colon would signify.

The Dry Salvages closes on a quiet note of secure commitment and assured direction that sets the stage for *Little Gidding's* Pentecostal climax.

❧ 4 ❧

Little Gidding

1 Midwinter spring is its own season
2 Sempiternal though sodden towards sundown,
3 Suspended in time, between pole and tropic.
4 When the short day is brightest, with frost and fire,
5 The brief sun flames the ice, on pond and ditches,
6 In windless cold that is the heart's heat,
7 Reflecting in a watery mirror
8 A glare that is blindness in the early afternoon.
9 And glow more intense than blaze of branch or brazier,
10 Stirs the dumb spirit: no wind, but pentecostal fire
11 In the dark time of the year. Between melting and freezing
12 The soul's sap quivers. There is no earth smell
13 Or smell of living thing. This is the spring time
14 But not in time's covenant. Now the hedgerow
15 Is blanched for an hour with transitory blossom
16 Of snow, a bloom more sudden
17 That that of summer, neither budding nor fading,
18 Not in the scheme of generation.
19 Where is the summer, the unimaginable
20 Zero summer?

Nᴏᴛ ᴀ ɴᴏᴛᴀʙʟᴇ ꜰᴇᴀᴛᴜʀᴇ, but a curious one, of *Little Gidding* is the relative difficulty with which the first part of the opening section is read aloud. The *s*-alliteration alone is hardly responsible, but the *s*-sequence is continually being interrupted by *p*'s and *t*'s with *b* and *f* entering the lists in the fourth line. The enforced slowness of enunciation gives a

simulated weight to syllables whose vowels are predominantly short and high, as in the first line up to the last two words
(such a run of identical vowels is uncommon).

The diction throughout is deceptively simple—many short
words in themselves or in other contexts unexciting, but
here combined to best advantage for exhibiting the desired
tensions. Between "Midwinter spring" (1) and "Zero
summer" (20) there are many similar word pairings, some
parallel and others (especially in the latter part) reversing the
order of the contrasted concepts:

1	Midwinter spring
3	pole and tropic
4	frost and fire
5	sun . . . ice
6	cold . . . heat
10-11	fire . . . dark time
11	melting and freezing
16-17	snow . . . summer
(17	budding nor fading)

The entire passage shows a preponderance of words
associated with light and heat. In addition to the appropriate
halves of the pairs already isolated we find "day," "brightest"
(4), "flames" (5), "Reflecting" (and "mirror") (7), "glare" (8),
"glow," "blaze," "brazier" (9). (Of incidental interest is the
fact that air and earth are denied consideration—"windless"
[6], "no wind" [10], "no earth smell" [12]—and water is
admitted only in a changed state, as the "watery mirror" [7]
of "ice, on pond and ditches" [5], or the "transitory
blossom/Of snow" [15-16].) Of two other series one deals
with time: "Midwinter spring," "season" (1), "Sempiternal,"
"sundown" (2), "Suspended in time" (3), "short" (4), "brief"
(5), "early afternoon" (8), "dark time of the year" (11),
"spring time" (13), "not in time's covenant," "Now" (14), "for
an hour," "transitory" (15), "sudden" (16), "summer" (17, 19,
20).

Without repeating the season terms or discounting those
prefixed by negatives we can list a similar group of words or
phrases relating to life or growth: "heart's heat" (6), "Stirs
the dumb spirit" (10), "soul's sap quivers" (12), "[no] smell of
living things," "blossom" (15), "bloom" (16), "neither budding

nor fading" (17), "Not in the scheme of generation" (18). (We might add "hedgerow" [14] as living.) In this last category the first three members are largely figurative, two others ("bloom" and "blossom") are entirely so, and the rest are specified as absent. "Neither budding nor fading" (17) has a curious ambiguity of its own. After grouping it with the heat-light versus cold-dark pairs by virtue of the dependence in the first place of "budding" upon a measure of heat and light, we realize that "fading" is caused by an excess of the same factors, while, as far as heat is concerned, (quick) freezing preserves (by arresting organic processes) as truly as frost blackens. Freezing (see also "melting and freezing" above [11]) can therefore be characterized as a neutral state rather than an extreme, and its immobility has affinities with the neither-nor qualities of the "still point." Since snow is the bloom "neither budding nor fading" in the life-and-growth group we are led to consider what it does instead—it simply comes, from the air, and vanishes, into water, or, if under certain conditions it sublimes (evaporates without first melting), into the air again (and into the air eventually anyway). Thus we find we are dealing with cycles and not with extremes (and this is true of the entire set of weather-and-season analogies) and with a kind of transmutation of (the four) elements with fire in the ascendancy, as suits the element that tends to turn what it touches into itself, and as accords with the Heraclitean formula with which the *Quartets* were prefaced.

Reduced to simplest terms these opening lines of *Little Gidding* are about the weather, an intense personal reaction that may be taken as part of it (and here is all the immediacy of *Burnt Norton* I; *East Coker* and *The Dry Salvages* were more briefly allusive in the personal bearing of their first sections), and a keen and moving historical memory that becomes explicit in the "broken king" line of the next strophe. The stirring of the spirit that anticipates the quickening of the life hidden in the soil has its counterpart (again the microcosm-macrocosm note) in the sudden thaw and the wind's stillness and the brilliance of high noon in an icy landscape. This is the poet's prompting, too, with the pentecostal gift of tongues to the "dumb spirit" (10), mightier than the glowing brazier redolent of sacrificial incense. The "transitory blossom / Of

snow" is appropriate to the anniversary of the beheading of
Charles I (January 30, 1649). We are told that "on the day of
his burial snow fell and the black pall was turned to white—a
sign of his innocence."[1] The word "covenant" (14) takes on
an added significance with the approach of the Puritan
regicides. The summer sought (19-20) with its strange
adjectives, whether or not it has, as has been suggested,[2] any
relation to absolute zero, represents an absolute in
experience, perhaps the "still point" again.

The syntactical organization of the first twenty lines of
Little Gidding is interesting for its balance. The statement of
line 1 could stand by itself. The modifiers of its subject (or of
its predicate nominative) each occupy a full line in which the
initial word is the main adjective (or participle)—"Sempiternal," "Suspended"—the next two words form a phrase
qualifying the adjective—"though sodden," "in time"—and
the remaining words constitute a prepositional phrase
standing in adverbial relation to the nearest participle—in
line 2 "sodden" thus intrudes on the preëminence of
"Sempiternal." The manner of application of these sub-
modifiers challenges investigation. What is the implicit
contrast between sempiternity and soddenness that inter-
poses "though" between them? The presence of the latter
quality hardly makes an end of spring. Essentially transient,
this "Midwinter spring" can be "Sempiternal" either insofar
as it is identifiable with the "timeless moment" or as
inevitably recurring. "Suspended in time" favors the former.
The adverbial phrases in 2 and 3 are respectively of time,
"towards sundown," and of place, "between pole and tropic."
The latter may be thought of as fixing the latitude (but in
terms of literally all-inclusive limits!) of this everlasting
spring as appropriately between unending winter and eternal
summer. "Suspended in time" shades into "by suspension of
time" on a seasonal scale without denying the change of day
into night indicated by "towards sundown." We seem by a
modification of Josue's miracle to have stopped the
revolution of the earth while permitting its continued
rotation.

The next sentence extends over five lines and is the last
for the present to end with the end of a line. Its main clause

is as brief and factual as that of the preceding sentence, but it is surrounded by a chain of linked dependencies that join the main stream of imagery to ensure the logical continuity as well as the thematic unity of the passage. Thus the temporal clause of line 4, "When the short day is brightest," with its superlative qualified "with frost and fire," is a real *amplificatio* preceding the basic "brief sun flames the ice." The phrase "on pond and ditches" can locate "the ice" despite the comma which separates them but which may mark only a rhetorical pause, or look to "frost and fire" above which it exactly parallels in line position, metrical make-up and grammatical form. Line 6 begins as the four preceding lines have ended, with a prepositional phrase (having a single object like that of line 2 instead of the paired nouns of the phrases between the first and last). "In windless cold" while it actually modifies the main verb, "flames," seems to share the loosely and transferrably dependent existence of the terminal phrases of 4 and 5. "That is the heart's heat" calls attention to its paradoxical equivalence with the "windless cold" by the juxtaposition of the final stresses, their near identity to the eye, and the speech effort demanded by the successive aspirates. Just how the relationship "cold . . . is . . . heat" is envisioned is matter for speculation. The possibilities include bitter irony, unlikely in the context, amounting to denial of the second term, and the more plausible transfiguration of the first term in what for want of a better word we can call the state of inspiration "heart's heat" denotes. "Reflecting . . ." (7) can logically modify only "ice" in line 5, while the object of this present participle, the "glare" that is [i.e., means, produces the effect of] blindness in the early afternoon [when the effect is at its height in contrast with its spent condition "towards sundown" (2)]," tends to ride over the period and reinforce its meaning with the "glow more intense . . ." which however is in syntactical fact the subject of the next sentence, and, after the alliterating and even rhyming comparison ("than blaze of branch or brazier"), "Stirs the dumb spirit." "No wind, but pentecostal fire" after a colon that bids pause (its normal prose function would make the wind and fire an enumeration under the heading "spirit," an interesting conjecture as far as the words are concerned but hardly feasible as prescinding entirely from the sense of the lines) would further explain the "glow" in a loosely appositive manner. Perhaps the rejection of the wind is necessary for the sake of the silence which is intense throughout the passage—the only possible sound is in the remote comparison "than blaze of branch" which would conceivably be accompanied by crackling; the weather is not such as to affect more than the surface of the ice which later may break up audibly. "In the dark time of the year" emphasizes the contrast, as it were between nature and grace, of the sudden illumination with its unpromising milieu.

From 11 to 14 there are three short sentences running mid-line to mid-line and revealing the characteristic carrying over of the same word—"smell," "time"-"time's."[3] They convey thereby a sense of breathlessness but without the foreboding that the many links between this poem and *Murder in the Cathedral* might bring with them. The introduction to *Little Gidding* telescopes—and with the difference in magnitude is a corresponding diminution of the prevailing tone of the play; in the poem the sense of liberation far exceeds that of oppression—the chant of the Chorus which has "seen these things in a shaft of sunlight:"[4] "not a stir, not a shoot.... Still and stifling the air: but a wind is stored up in the East."[5] Another and a startling difference transforms the speech of the First Tempter: "Spring has come in winter. Snow in the branches/Shall float as sweet as blossoms. Ice along the ditches/Mirror the sunlight. Love in the orchard/Send the sap shooting."[6] Kinship is reaffirmed in the pilgrimage references in the third part of *Little Gidding* I, "You are here to kneel/Where prayer has been valid" (47-48), and in the final chorus of *Murder in the Cathedral*, "wherever a saint has dwelt...There is holy ground and sanctity shall not depart from it...."[7]

"Now the hedgerow...," a four-and-a-half-line sentence (14-18), returns to the strung-out syntax of the earlier part of the passage; "blossom" (15), the object in the prepositional phrase that serves the main verb ("Is blanched" [15]) as a kind of ablative of cause, bears the weight of the next three lines including an appositive ("bloom") lengthened by a completed comparison ("more sudden/Than that of summer" [16-17]), a two-fold participial modifier ("neither budding nor fading" [17]), and a final prepositional phrase containing still another ("Not in the scheme of generation" [18]).

We end on a question whose answer will break on the reader toward the poem's close.

The second (typographically distinct) portion of *Little Gidding* I was anticipated phrasally to some degree by *East Coker* 135ff.[8]

21   If you came this way,
22   Taking the route you would be likely to take
23   From the place you would be likely to come from
24   If you came this way in may time, you would find the hedges
25   White again, in May, with voluptuary sweetness.
26   It would be the same at the end of the journey,
27   If you came at night like a broken king,
28   If you came by day not knowing what you came for,
29   It would be the same, when you leave the rough road
30   And turn behind the pig-sty to the dull façade
31   And the tombstone. And what you thought you came for
32   Is only a shell, a husk of meaning
33   From which the purpose breaks only when it is fulfilled
34   If at all. Either you had no purpose
35   Or the purpose is beyond the end you figured
36   And is altered in fulfilment. There are other places
37   Which are also the world's end, some at the sea jaws,
38   Or over a dark lake, in a desert or a city—
39   But this is the nearest, in place and time,
40   Now and in England.

We are on the same road as in the first twenty lines, with the same hedgerow, but the season is the natural spring, with hawthorne instead of snow whitening the way. Legend and folk custom and superstitution cling to may blossom, but this rich deposit provides general resonance rather than particular evocation here. Line 21 in a sense completes 20 metrically, but it opens a new phase of the journey with the double envelope refrains of which it is the recurring component:

21 If you came
22 you would be likely
23 you would be likely
24 If you came

26 It would be the same
27 If you came
28 If you came
29 It would be the same

Other refrain-like repetitions include: "may"-"May" (24-25), "what you came for" (28)-"what you thought you came for"(31), "purpose" (33, 34, 35), "fulfilled" (33)-"fulfillment" (36), "end of the journey" (26)-"beyond the end" (35)-"the world's end" (37). The keynote here is "purpose"—it enters into all the above except the "may" pair. We are still trying to cope with experience and its meaning. Turned every way it still eludes us—"at night," "by day," "It would be the same," and along the hedges' "voluptuary sweetness" and before "the dull façade / And the tombstone." Is there a hint of the Prodigal in the association of "husk" and "pig-sty," especially with journey and failure in the background? In any event the purpose is fulfilled by the stripping off of what would deceive.

"Other places" where eternal purposes have seen fulfilment in holy lives were given at greater length in *Murder in the Cathedral*: "From where the western seas gnaw at the coast of Iona, / To the death in the desert, the prayer in forgotton places by the broken inperial column."[9] If "the sea jaws" are Iona, "a dark lake" could be Subiaco, "a desert" that of the Fathers (or of Browning's St. John the Evangelist) and "a city" any of those in the *Acts of the Apostles* that was the scene of a communal gathering of early Christians. Inverse chronology and some similarity of purpose lessen the seeming extravagance of placing Nicholas Ferrar at the culmination of the line traced through Saints Columba, Benedict, Paul and Anthony and the very Apostles. There is pathos rather in Eliot's clinging to Little Gidding as "the nearest, in place and time" and sympathies.

The third part of *Little Gidding* I opens with the same words and line arrangement that began the second, and ends with a variation on its closing phrase. It is summary (through

44 middle) and development and explanation of the foregoing while it relates the themes of purpose and prayer, language and tradition with the moment of heightened awareness that is the central experience of the poem.

41   If you came this way,
42 Taking any route, starting from anywhere,
43 At any time or at any season,
44 It would always be the same: you would have to put
   off
45 Sense and notion. You are not here to verify,
46 Instruct yourself, or inform curiosity
47 Or carry report. You are here to kneel
48 Where prayer has been valid. And prayer is more
49 Than an order of words, the conscious occupation
50 Of the praying mind, or the sound of the voice
   praying.
51 And what the dead had no speech for, when living,
52 They can tell you, being dead: the communication
53 Of the dead is tongued with fire beyond the
   language of the living.
54 Here, the intersection of the timeless moment
55 Is England and nowhere. Never and always.

We are to "put off / Sense and notion" (44-45) just as in *East Coker* we had to "Wait without thought" (*EC* 128) and "go by the way of dispossession" (*EC* 143). The shift in mood assumes our compliancy—"If you came...you would have to," "You are ...here" ("not" in 45 is considered as modifying the infinitive and not the adverb it precedes). It is not "the knowledge derived from experience" (*EC* 84) which is to be sought or valued here, but a submission of intellect which surrenders even the discursive forms of prayer. 51-53 belong not with *Dry Salvages* 188, "To...converse with spirits," but with "the experience...of many generations" (*DS* 100-101) and still more to the doctrine of the communion of saints. Literary remains one feels to be out of the question for this particular "communication / Of the Dead" (52-53). This is the wisdom "Which shall fructify in the lives of others" (*DS* 162).

The last two lines of the section are syntactically of peculiar formation. "Here," set off by a comma from the rest of 54, can refer back to the Anglican shrine "Where prayer

has been valid" (48), or ahead to the body of its own line—
the absence of another comma at the end of 54 does not deny
to "the intersection..." an appositive function explanatory of
"Here." This "intersection" is logically incomplete, having an
"of" term but no "with." It is equated directly with "England
and nowhere" (55); time, or the timeless, *is* place, not
localized *in* place, and, in the same breath, is placeless. After a
full stop "Never and always" (55) strike the final chord of
timeless and eternal as qualities befitting this intricately told
transcendence by the spirit of man of the space-time
continuum which frames his earthly existence.

Little Gidding II like the other second sections is partly
stanzaic and rhymed and partly, though with a difference,
"plain." The unrhymed longer portion (80-151) is indented[10]
in three's and is obviously intended to suggest (and has been
generally recognized as so doing) Dante's *terza rima.*
We begin with the element stanzas:

56 Ash on an old man's sleeve
57 Is all the ash the burnt roses leave.
58 Dust in the air suspended
59 Marks the place where a story ended.
60 Dust inbreathed was a house—
61 The wall, the wainscot and the mouse.
62 The death of hope and despair,
63   This is the death of air.

64   There are flood and drouth
65 Over the eyes and in the mouth,
66 Dead water and dead sand
67 Contending for the upper hand.
68 The parched eviscerate soil
69 Gapes at the vanity of toil,
70 Laughs without mirth.
71   This is the death of earth.

72   Water and fire succeed
73 The town, the pasture and the weed.
74 Water and fire deride
75 The sacrifice that we denied.
76 Water and fire shall rot
77 The marred foundations we forgot,

78 Of sanctuary and choir.
79   This is the death of water and fire.

There is an overlapping of objects from the earlier *Quartets* which are presented here as the prey of mutability. In the first stanza we recognize *Burnt Norton's* roses and "the wall, the wainscot and the mouse" of *East Coker*, in the second, *East Coker's* earth and the water and sand of *The Dry Salvages*, and in the third, while "Water and fire" are proper respectively to *The Dry Salvages* and *Little Gidding*, we meet *East Coker* again in "The town, the pasture and the weed." But there is a new note, too, in stanza three, with the first and only occurrence in the *Quartets* of the word "sacrifice." This with "The marred foundations... /Of sanctuary and choir" (77-78)[11] (although these last could, to be sure, have incurred damage during the air raids subsequently alluded to) has a definite pre-Reformation ring. Eliot's known admiration for the Caroline divines extends to their efforts to ward off from Anglo-Catholicism some of the protestantizing tendencies he and they deplore.

The stanza scheme is basically $a_3a_4b_3b_4c_3c_4d_3d_3$ or $_4$ but in some instances one of the stresses is suppressed (as falling on "and" in 73, or the last syllable of "vanity" in 69, and in 64 where "There are" might be scanned as an example of hovering stress).

The most provocative word in the first stanza is the second "the" in the second line. Rhythmically *de trop*—"burnt" is too long to be slurred with it to fit between accented "ash" and "roses"—it is puzzling for the sense as well, making the "burnt roses" uncomfortably particular. The roses of *Burnt Norton* I that were an integral part of the garden experience were the living ones, but there was also "the dust on a bowl of rose-leaves" (*BN* 17) which it was to no purpose to disturb. By *Little Gidding* these too are fire-touched, and whether incense of prayer or holocaust of memory their spent fragrance joins the patriarchal "dust and ashes" (*Genesis* 18:27) that pleaded for Sodom before the fire from heaven descended. Dust motes are all that are left of merely human fears and aspirations, while the end of human discourse is signalized only by a cessation of disturbance of the air.

Each pair of lines in the first stanza is a complete

sentence. In the *a* and *b* couplets the subject and its phrase modifier occupy the first line and the predicate with its modifying clause the second. The *c* couplet offers a syntactically full first line with the second merely amplifying (by enumeration of parts—if the mouse too may be so designated) the subjective complement, "house." The *d* couplet reverses this procedure, its first line expanding (by repetition with a difference, the "of" phrase in 62 functioning as a subjective genitive while that in 63 could be called a genitive of specification) the real subject, "death," of the concluding line-statement. The noun series "Ash"-"ash," "Dust"-"Dust," "death"-"death" is equally symmetrical, the *a* couplet containing the "ash" pair, the *d* couplet the "death," while "Dust" occurs in the first lines of the two inner couplets. Pattern is more than ever evident in the shaping of these lines.[12]

The only exact repetition in the second stanza is the twice applied adjective "dead" in its third line (66), but a fairly constant ratio exists between the paired terms of 64-66 which are in some way opposed if not true opposites: "flood and drouth," "eyes and...mouth," "water and...sand." Echoes here from the early Eliot are strong. We think of the "old man in a dry month"[13] and the corpse planted in the garden.[14] "Flood and drouth" of seasons rainy and dry are among the few vicissitudes that touch the grave's tenant. Blind and speechless, here truly does one "put off/Sense and notion" (44-45). "Dead" fitly describes the water and sand that seep into a coffin and blocks out another image of a body cast up and reclaimed by the almost living tide on the beach of *The Dry Salvages.* 68 sounds like a real Waste Land whose sterility mocks the would-be cultivator (and contrasts with the more positive note of *EC* 39-40). Exhausted and lifeless, it is no longer capable of giving life. "This is the death of earth" in the sense of earth's dying, too.

"Water and fire" form a true refrain in the third stanza, beginning its first, third and fifth lines and ending its last. The only aspect of these elements presented here is the destructive one; they sweep all before them, starting with that which most shows the hand of man, "The town" (73), then "the pasture" and finally "the weed" whose encroachment has itself challenged man's dominion. The despoilers mock our pusillanimity (74-78) and we are the losers altogether where we might have merited spiritually. The justice of the Noahs and Abrahams does not suspend this exercise of the divine vengeance in "the death of water and fire" and cataclysmic warfare.

The triplet portion of *Little Gidding* II is unique in the *Quartets* for its sustained narrative-plus-dialogue structure, built of long and regular syntactic units prosodically and tonally close to traditional non-dramatic blank verse with a fairly free disposition of stresses and a—doubtless intentional—leaning toward a hendecasyllabic line. It is the alternation of masculine and feminine end-words that is largely responsible for the a-b-a, b-c-b, c-d-c effect.

In the diction we are not done with paradox, as "the ending of interminable night" (81) and "the recurrent end of the unending" (82) testify, but it is here more rhetorical device than challenge to delve for hidden meanings. Metaphor and simile too are more than usually prominent in the first sentence.

80   In the uncertain hour before the morning
81   Near the ending of interminable night
82   At the recurrent end of the unending
83 After the dark dove with the flickering tongue
84   Had passed below the horizon of his homing
85   While the dead leaves still rattled on like tin
86 Over the asphalt where no other sound was
87   Between three districts whence the smoke
         arose
88   I met one walking, loitering and hurried
89 As if blown towards me like the metal leaves
90   Before the urban dawn wind unresisting.

Among the first things we notice are the unit quality of the lines which renders end punctuation unnecessary and the abundance of prepositional phrases devoted to the exact timing and placing of the simple core "I met one" (88). Six of the ten lines begin so—"In the" (80), "Near the" (81), "At the " (82), "Over the" (86), "Between" (87), "Before the" (90)— and two of the others substitute conjunctions to much the same effect—"After the" (83), "While the" (85). Seven of the lines (80-85, 89) contain prepositional phrases in other than initial positions (and introduced in part by the quieter prepositions, "of" and "with"). 86 and 87 offer brief and specific adverbial clauses with "where" and "whence" respectively.

The setting for this crucial encounter is an admirable blend of realistic suggestion and supernatural detail. The bomber has returned whence it came after a chastening visitation which leaves the solitary warden both numb and alert with the quickend senses and impotence to act of one emerging from anaesthesia. The "uncertain hour before the morning," the smoking reminders of the experience just undergone, the place "Between three districts" and in none of them, all conspire to raise the ghost whose coming is heralded by the "metal leaves" so reminiscent of those Aeneas sought as passport to his converse with the dead—"sic leni crepitabat brattea vento" (*Aeneid* VI, 209). Eliot's "loitering and hurried" (88) photograph with the utmost economy the approach of the visitant.

> 91   And as I fixed upon the down-turned face
> 92 That pointed scrutiny with which we challenge
> 93   The first-met stranger in the waning dusk
> 94   I caught the sudden look of some dead master
> 95 Whom I had known, forgotten, half recalled
> 96   Both one and many; in the brown baked features
> 97   The eyes of a familiar compound ghost
> 98 Both intimate and unidentifiable.

The *Inferno* parallel (Canto XV) of this encounter has had frequent comment, but after the phrasal clues of "pointed scrutiny...in the waning dusk" and the "baked features" and "are *you* here" we must beware of too close identification of Eliot's mentor with any single counterpart of Brunetto Latini, for this "familiar compound ghost," "Both one and many," is purposely so described.

A loosening of syntax is noticeable after the middle of 95—"forgotten, half recalled" do not correspond in function with "known" just before them, but go back to "some dead master" in the preceding line. "Half recalled" is indeed ready to abandon the role of participle for that of finite verb, with potential subjects in the pronoun of "I caught" (94) and, quite strongly, in "the sudden look," while "Both one and many" is as serviceable as object of "recalled" in either function as its pronominal adjectives are as modifiers or appositives of "some dead master." The ellipsis of 96 middle to 98 succeeds in being unobtrusive, and we readily supply "were" before 97 or echo "I caught the sudden look of." The recognition of the "intimate and unidentifiable" is of a piece with the other elusive *reconnaissances* of the *Quartets* from *BN*'s presences.

99   So I assumed a double part, and cried
100   And heard another's voice cry: 'What! are *you* here?'
101 Although we were not. I was still the same,
102   Knowing myself yet being someone other—
103   And he a face still forming; yet the words sufficed
104 To compel the recognition they preceded.
105   And so, compliant to the common wind,
106   Too strange to each other for misunderstanding,
107 In concord at this intersection time
108   Of meeting nowhere, no before and after,
109   We trod the pavement in a dead patrol.

Without positing a supranormal psychological state one can envision such a projection, real to the *eidetiker* but imaginatively within reach of most. The slight confusion incident to this displacing of the ordinary limits of personality is reflected in 103 which can be read either as an alexandrine or with hypermetric slacks after the semi-colon. Otherwise there is no perceptible break in the smoothly fluent rhythmic and verbal current whose movement from the first (80) has been quietly supported by lettering devices which lie for the most part just beneath the surface of conscious articulation. Such include the close alliterations, "dark dove" (83), "horizon of his homing" (84), "brown baked" (97); the repeated syllable in "ending"-"end"-"unending" (81-82) and "compel"-"compliant"-"common" (104-105), "nowhere, no" (108); and miscellaneous word series like "blown"-"dawn"-"down" (89-91), "dawn wind"-"waning dusk" (90-93), "trod...pavement"-"patrol" (109). The soft *f*'s which cluster in 95-97—"forgotten, half," "features," "familiar," "unidentifiable"—gather anew in company with sibilants in 102-103—"Myself," "face still forming," "sufficed."

The introductory narrative begins and ends with advertence to the problem of time and the timeless, from the "end of the unending" (82) to "no before and after" (108). Place too is transcended at the latter end, "meeting nowhere" now although the asphalt pavement was previously localized with deliberate exactness (86-87). The protagonist prompts the other's remarks:

110 I said: 'The wonder that I feel is easy,
111   Yet ease is cause of wonder. Therefore speak:
112   I may not comprehend, may not remember.'

Brevity does not mean stylistic sacrifice—"wonder...is easy"-"ease is...wonder" (110-111) alternate word order without change of stress; "may not"-"may not" (112) maintain word order but reverse stress if the iambic pattern is considered to obtain here.

The spirit dismisses the past as though temporal sequence were a significant factor in evaluating experience, an apparent departure, fortified by the homely imagery of 118-119, from one of the basic themes.

113 And he: 'I am not eager to rehearse
114   My thought and theory which you have forgot-
         ten.
115   These things have served their purpose: let them
         be.
116 So with your own, and pray they be forgiven
117   By others, as I pray you to forgive
118   Both bad and good. Last season's fruit is eaten
119 And the fullfed beast shall kick the empty pail.
120   For last year's words belong to last year's
         language
121   And next year's words await another voice.

This, however, is qualified at once in the actual blending of "two worlds" neither of which seems thoroughly infernal but whose relationship is rather like that depicted in Charles Williams' *All Hallows' Eve* (for which novel Eliot provided an introduction) where the purgatorial half-world lies all about us and contacts are possible to the properly attuned.

122 But, as the passage now presents no hindrance

123   To the spirit unappeased and peregrine
124   Between two worlds become much like each
        other,
125 So I find words I never thought to speak
126   In streets I never thought I should revisit
127   When I left my body on a distant shore.

The patterns are phrasal (120-121, 125-126) and alliterative, as in *p, l* and *w*—without going farther back we find "last"-"belong"-"last"-"language" (120), "words"-"words"-"await" (120-121), "passage"-"presents"-("spirit")-"unappeased"-"peregrine" (122-123). Vowel groups are less conspicuous save for the concentration of long *ee* sounds (123ff.)—"unapp*ee*ased," "per*e*gr*i*ne," "Betw*ee*n," "*ea*ch," "sp*ea*k," "str*ee*ts," "sp*ee*ch" (twice). (This coincidence gives added prominence to the unusual "unappeased and peregrine" amid the otherwise rather pedestrian diction.)

128 Since our concern was speech, and speech impelled
        us
129   To purify the dialect of the tribe
130   And urge the mind to aftersight and foresight,
131 Let me disclose the gifts reserved for age
132   To set a crown upon your lifetime's effort.

The Mallarméen sentiment of 129 often echoed in a truly crusading spirit by Ezra Pound is also very much Eliot's own,[15] and is as much independent conviction as index of discipleship even in this master-pupil context. "After-sight and foresight" (130) accompany the Pandora "gifts reserved for age" (131) with all they recall of old men's "folly,/Their fear of fear and frenzy..." (*EC* 95-96).

133   First, the cold friction of expiring sense
134 Without enchantment, offering no promise
135   But bitter tastelessness of shadow fruit
136   As body and soul begin to fall asunder.
137 Second, the conscious impotence of rage
138   At human folly, and the laceration
139   Of laughter at what ceases to amuse.

These resemble the bitter reflections of *Gerontion* and the fruits of his rejections, but there are other relations, e.g., the "wounded surgeon" section of *East Coker* and the mutability stanzas of *Little Gidding* itself. The emphasis is not entirely on the physical aspects of death but these are natural symbols of the disintegration and disillusion which ironically "crown... [the] lifetime's effort" of the pure humanist who suffers in the *Dies irae* when "Quidquid latet apparebit" but whose mentality, untouched by faith in the Incarnation, perceives the merest glimmer of that restorative "refining fire." This voice of one come from the dead directs indeed toward "the still point, [where] the dance is" but the sombre message of the uneasy spirit warns of the barrenness of such achievement as has been his and as that to which the disciple seems to aspire in the "language" parts of the poem.

140 And last, the rending pain of re-enactment
141   Of all that you have done, and been; the shame
142   Of motives late revealed, and the awareness
143 Of things ill done and done to others' harm
144   Which once you took for exercise of virtue.
145   Then fools' approval stings, and honour stains.
146 From wrong to wrong the exasperated spirit
147   Proceeds, unless restored by that refining fire
148   Where you must move in measure, like a dancer.

In these last lines a certain couplet quality is suggested by the greater end-stopping and the Popean balance of, for example, 143 and 145.

Like others of his kind the ghost must go before the day comes, and does so duly "on the blowing of the horn." The latest associations (from *Hamlet* and *Purgatorio* XXVI) are not with damned souls but with those whose suffering is in hope. The progression recapitulates the tenor of the whole Eliot canon.

The concluding lines of *Little Gidding* II are themselves a valediction closing a passage of profound realization quietly unfolded in a parable of experience. The control of language is such that even the well worn "poetic" first half of 149 has all the impact of its original freshness. "Disfigured" in the same line pricks our attention in case it has flagged, and sends us looking into its possible and simultaneous extraordinary meanings of "unpeopled" and, taking "figure" as an element of design, "unpatterned."

149 The day was breaking. In the disfigured street
150   He left me, with a kind of valediction,
151   And faded on the blowing of the horn.

The two parts of *Little Gidding* III contrast in line length—
152-167 use a free and occasionally dubious five-stress line
(155 and 166 break into two three-stress halves) while 168-
210 are predominantly three-stressed. Tonally however they
are not so far apart as the first line of each might suggest;
after the drily enumerative start of 152, threatening hair-
splitting, and the simple but sweeping paradox of Juliana of
Norwich in 168, we find a real similarity in the repetitive
phrasing and characteristic rhetoric of a reflective stamp.
This circumstance of difference with sameness may remind
us of the two schools of western spirituality, the elaborate
and "scientific" seventeenth century French systems fathered
on their Spanish forebears and the homely and childlike
fourteenth century English mysticism, which are after all one
in aim and guide the same human nature to its higher
realizations. The sampling Eliot gives us here and elsewhere
is less the early restless eclecticism than a catholicity in
which Buddha and Heraclitus and St. John of the Cross are
all at home, not as in a pantheon or a museum but as seen
through a light filter which transmits from the greater and
lesser bodies those rays of common truth their facets reflect.

The first sentence of the section makes a show of clarity:

152 There are three conditions which often look alike
153 Yet differ completely, flourish in the same hedge-
    row:
154 Attachment to self and to things and to persons,
    detachment
155 From self and from things and from persons; and,
    growing between them, indifference
156 Which resembles the others as death resembles life,
157 Being between two lives—unflowering, between
158 The live and the dead nettle.

A slight syntactical peculiarity is the placing of "flourish
in the same hedgerow" (153) which in sense and line position
parallels "often look alike" (152) but which expectation
prompted by normal word-order (so far not departed from)

would relate to "differ completely." The tension thus set up
is a little like the return after an interruption to an absorbing
notion fed by rumination. Again, "Attachment" and
"detachment" begin and end the same line (154) as if to
emphasize their polarity (as allowing "detachment" to begin
the next line, directly under "Attachment," would not).
"Indifference," the third condition, is appropriately an end
word like "detachment" (to which it is closer), although
typographically (in *CPP*), line 155 having overflowed its
bounds, it is actually "between them."

    154 Attachment   detachment
    155   indifference

Under deceiving appearances attachment may masquerade as
selfless devotion. Detachment in its positive aspect is the
strongest of attachments as its object, union with God, is the
greatest that can attract the human will. Indifference (not
the holy kind) is a travesty of the negative side of genuine
detachment. It is therefore to the two types of vigorous
activity to which it is compared as death is to life, and like
death, unproductive, "unflowering" (157). "The live and the
dead nettle" (158), though, are offered as exemplifying the
"two lives" (157), respectively, those of attachment and
detachment. The nature of the stinging nettle is perhaps the
clue to its choice in what is not a contradiction but a form of
conceptual zeugma (in the seemingly incompatible ways in
which "death" and "dead" are applied as the figure develops).
The spines are as prickly in the living and dead specimens,
but the former may communicate a poison also. Thus,
though both can be painful, attachment might be insidiously
harmful. (On the other hand, a well ordered love of creatures
is a way to God; this view rather than the negative one is
given greater prominence in the poem.)

    158   This is the use of memory:
    159 For liberation—not less of love but expanding
    160 Of love beyond desire, and so liberation
    161 From the future as well as the past. Thus, love of a
        country
    162 Begins as attachment to our own field of action
    163 And comes to find that action of little importance

164 Though never indifferent. History may be servitude,
165 History may be freedom. See, now they vanish,
166 The faces and places, with the self which, as it
could, loved them,
167 To become renewed, transfigured, in another
pattern.

The connection of these lines with the foregoing is at first obscure, especially as regards the role of "memory" (158). The difficulty is really one arising from extreme compression. We seem to need to expand "use" (158) into a periphrasis like "avoidance of abuse" (for memory wrongfully exercised is a form of attachment to the past) and then contract it to its original curt limits which make memory properly used a positive force "For liberation" (159). With anxiety, seen as a form of attachment to the future, and involving speculation as well as emotion, we add the faculty of understanding to memory and will in this concurrence of the powers of the soul in our purification or undoing.

As it is time, "the future as well as the past" (161), that we are freed from in the "memory" sentence, so next our local attachments are ennobled into patriotism (as honoring an ideal, not as exalting a nationality; true *pietas*). "History" (164, 165) combines time and place and enshrines the ideal, attachment to which (good end but bad means) is "servitude" (164) while detachment ("Though never indifferen[ce]") is "freedom" (165). "Now" (165), with this realization full upon us, the "faces and places" (166), the persons and things and the self which has put away its disordered love of creatures, are restored in the liberating "pattern" that (*BN* 143-145) made for the "stillness" of perfect detachment and the measured "dance" of perfect ordering of the affections. Is it fanciful to see in these last three lines an enlarged picture of the close of the last section? There the one "restored by that refining fire" (147), who shortly before had been only "a face still forming" (103), "faded" (151) out of sight "In the disfigured street" (149). Here "faces" (166) and all their associations "vanish" (165) "To become renewed, trans-figured" (167). If the links are more than verbal the story of the second section may well be an *exemplum*.

"All shall be well" is the reiterated cry of Mother Juliana's portion of Section III. History's "cunning passages, contrived corridors" (*Gerontion* 36 [*CPP*, p. 22]) unwind to a *felix culpa*— "Sin is Behovely" (168); "all time is eternally present" (*BN* 4) and is now redeemed.

168   Sin is Behovely, but
169 All shall be well, and
170 All manner of thing shall be well.
171 If I think, again, of this place,
172 And of people, not wholly commendable,
173 Of no immediate kin or kindness,
174 But some of peculiar genius,
175 All touched by a common genius,
176 United in the strife which divided them;
177 If I think of a king at nightfall,
178 Of three men, and more, on the scaffold
179 And a few who died forgotten
180 In other places, here and abroad,
181 And of one who died blind and quiet,
182 Why should we celebrate
183 These dead men more than the dying?

Ferrar's community, the rule of those other "saints," and the lot of their victims give pause for thought. The pastness of the events reviewed does not render them the less contemporaneous. Bygones have become part of the timeless pattern. There is scope here for a typological view of history, both in the interrelation of purely human and natural events and in the muted Passion reference of the scaffold line.

External syntactical arrangement has its limitations as a guide in excerpting in this section. 182-183 while technically needed to complete the sentence which began in 171 belong in thought to the next three lines (184-186), which the three following (187-189) further explicate before the resolution of 194-197 and recapitulation of the opening chord, with embellishment, in 198-201.

184 It is not to ring the bell backward
185 Nor is it an incantation
186 To summon the spectre of a Rose.
187 We cannot revive old factions

188 We cannot restore old policies
189 Or follow an antique drum.
190 These men, and those who opposed them
191 And those whom they opposed
192 Accept the constitution of silence
193 And are folded in a single party.
194 Whatever we inherit from the fortunate
195 We have taken from the defeated
196 What they had to leave us—a symbol:
197 A symbol perfected in death.
198 And all shall be well and
199 All manner of thing shall be well
200 By the purifcation of the motive
201 In the ground of our beseeching.

The rhetorical organization has then as outer limits the first and last line groups containing "All... All manner of thing shall be well." (Nor is the final weighted "and" of 169 and 198 insignificant or merely an expedient resorted to in the arrangement as verse of the original prose; it is both brake and pointer.) Two other units are identifiable as opening with "If I think" (171 and 177) and closing with lines of like vowels not elsewhere recurring save singly: "United in the strife which divided them" (176) and "And one who died blind and quiet" (181). The "If I think" lines follow a vowel pattern as well as a phrasal, each containing three short *i*'s ("If I think... this" [171], If I think... king" [177]) as against the three diphthongized *i*'s of their partners. Within each of these divisions there is a high degree of symmetrical subordination—the first "think" is completed by "of this place, / And of people" (171-172); the second by "of a king... / Of three men" (177-178). These last are particularized as to time, "at nightfall," and place, "on the scaffold," and added to by "more" (178), "And a few" (179), "and of one" (181), the two last having clause modifiers detailing their dying. The first "think" group is differently subdivided, with another pair of "of" phrases serving as genitives of description, each containing an internal contrast, in one instance a simple alternate object, "Of no immediate kin or kindness [in the sense of "nature," and more alliterative tag than contribution to meaning]" (173), and in the other a complex part-and-whole attribution of genius "peculiar" and "common" which leaves the original phrasal confines altogether in line 175, "All," like "some" (174), becoming an appositive of "people" (172). Between the two "think" groups there are verbal antinomies: "this place" (171)-"other places" (180), ("not wholly") "commendable" (172)-"forgotten" (179), "some...all" (174-175)-"more...few" (178-179), "United" (176)-"here and abroad" (180), "strife...divided" (176)-"died...quiet" (181).

Smaller groups include 187-188, "We cannot re-...old;" 190-191, "These...those...opposed"-"those...they opposed;" 194-196, "Whatever...from the fortunate"-"from the defeated/What;" to the last we might add the repeated "symbol" (196, 197) and relate the associated "death" (197) to the "dead men" coda to the two "think" units.

184-186 might be read with advertence to note 12, above, as well as to the ghost-raising of *Little Gidding* II and *East Coker* V. Diction of another flavor forms a thread through "old factions" (187), "old policies" (188) ("antique drum" [189]— note the syllabic arrangement; the concrete noun is now the monosyllable), "Accept the constitution" (192), "single party" (193), ("inherit" [194]).

194-197 are the key to the larger passage. The reconciliations effected in 190-193 represent a triumph of perspective. The detached observer may learn detachment of spirit. The symbol, be it of nobility or loyalty or self-sacrifice, is, as the legacy of the past to the future, the unifying element in the time scale and a means to its surmounting.

The concluding sentence (198-201) restates 169-170 but adds the condition of their realization. Simplicity of heart was urged in the detachment passage (152ff.); here is the purity of intention that must accompany it to make prayer "valid." The last two lines form another link with the earlier section where we read of "the shame/Of motives late revealed" (141-142). Again, "motive" ("motif") and "ground" describe a pattern, consistently of thematic moment in the *Quartets*.

The lyric fourth section is the briefest since *Burnt Norton's*. The two seven-line stanzas rhyme a-b-a-b-a-c-c with the last line a partial refrain. We have returned (more or less) to octosyllabics except in the third line of each stanza in which we have just three very distinct iambic feet.

202 The dove descending breaks the air
203 With flame of incandescent terror
204 Of which the tongues declare
205 The one discharge from sin and error.
206 The only hope, or else despair
207   Lies in the choice of pyre or pyre—
208   To be redeemed from fire by fire.

209   Who then devised the torment? Love.
210 Love is the unfamiliar Name
211 Behind the hands that wove
212 The intolerable shirt of flame.
213 Which human power cannot remove.
214   We only live, only suspire
215   Consumed by either fire or fire.

There is explicit recognition here of war as an instrument of divine chastisement. The departing raider seen as "the dark dove with the flickering tongue" (83) had disposed the watcher of section II to heed the monitions of one already judged. The return of the fire-laden plane reminds him of his own judgment and the choice open to him of purification by suffering here or hereafter. But this coming is the coming of the Spirit of Love and proceeds from the "absolute paternal care" and the "sharp compassion" of the surgeon's steel (*EC* IV). The Nessus shirt, bestowed not inflicted, becomes a condition of life, which would be a very writhing service of God if the pain were not transmuted into love and the fire thoroughly Teresian. (One would wish, parenthetically, that Eliot had dwelt more on the passage in à Kempis which tells us that "in the Cross is joy of spirit.")

The simplicity of the first stanza is perhaps artful. We wonder if the "terror"-"error" rhyme and "tongues declare" recall any particular Sunday school hymn. The last three lines of the stanza show interesting proportions of the alternatives given in the first of them: 206 is divided equally between "hope" and "despair"; 207 is three-fourths hope, only the last foot referring to the pyre of despair; in 208 despair has disappeared except as something to be redeemed from by another fire.

209 opens the second stanza with the rhetorical "Who then devised the torment?" and its all-sufficing answer, "Love." The adjective "unfamiliar" and the capitalized "Name" (210) are eloquent of the Unknown God. "Intolerable" carries with it its rare meaning of "irresistible" and possibly the obsolete "extreme."

The concluding section of *Little Gidding* and of the *Quartets* as a whole is all that we should expect as summation and resolution. The new combinations of old elements reveal surprising turns and connections; loose ends are tied into a veritable "crowned knot" (260) and the fire-fused images blend into as perfect a whole as can be achieved with the limited medium the poet uses here for the last time. Quite literally "every word is at home,/Taking its place to support the others" (219-220), for each word in itself contributes to the present context while many (as do many a phrase and an occasional entire line) bring also the full retinue of their original *Quartet* associations.

The typographical division that seems standard (that of *CPP*)[16] makes satisfactory quoting units.

216 What we call the beginning is often the end
217 And to make an end is to make a beginning.
218 The end is where we start from. And every phrase
219 And sentence that is right (where every word is at home,
220 Taking its place to support the others,
221 The word neither diffident nor ostentatious,
222 An easy commerce of the old and the new,
223 The common word exact without vulgarity,
224 The formal word precise but not pedantic,
225 The complete consort dancing together)
226 Every phrase and every sentence is an end and a beginning,
227 Every poem an epitaph. And any action
228 Is a step to the block, to the fire, down the sea's throat
229 Or to an illegible stone: and that is where we start.
230 We die with the dying:
231 See, they depart, and we go with them.
232 We are born with the dead:

233 See, they return, and bring us with them.
234 The moment of the rose and the moment of the
     yew-tree
235 Are of equal duration. A people without history
236 Is not redeemed from time, for history is a pattern
237 Of timeless moments. So, while the light fails
238 On a winter's afternoon, in a secluded chapel
239 History is now and England.
240 With drawing of this Love and the voice of this
     Calling

(Note that there is no end punctuation after 240; the sentence it begins continues into the lines which follow the break and which are syntactically quite capable of standing alone. The gap is rhetorically more effective—and more immediately so as a physical impression—than classical punctuation would be.)

"End" and "beginning" in line 216 take us back to *Burnt Norton* V and to the first and last lines of *East Coker*. The reversal of temporal values is now more nearly complete. In *EC* 192 "Home is where one starts from." Here "the end is where we start from." There is a certain consistency in this—"end" is "beginning" is "home." But we are not far from the recurring consideration of language as such— "phrase" and "sentence" are end and beginning in onflowing series and waxing "approach to the meaning" (*DS* 96). The "poem" is the culmination, and like "an epitaph" (227) confers a kind of permanence on what it celebrates at the same time as it testifies to its transience. The six and a half lines in parentheses (219 middle-225) are Eliot's prescription for rightness of style and diction and a standard against which his own performance in the *Quartets* may be measured with justice and admiration—" The common word exact without vulgarity, / The formal word precise but not pedantic" (223-224). But there are overtones larger than language; the "easy commerce of the old and the new" by the accident of a single word recalls the river god of *The Dry Salvages* with his degradation and resentment but above all his continuity and quasi-immortality; "The complete consort dancing together" (225) revives the symbolism of *East Coker* I (24ff.) where union and harmony were lifted from the physical to the spiritual plane. The sacramental nature of these words and things seems never foreign to Eliot's thought and use of them although it remains a deduction we must draw for ourselves.

From words we proceed to "action" (227). Krishna's syllogistic definitions (*DS* 158ff.)—intention at death is fruitful action, death is every moment, and, by implication and background, moments of "stillness" are fruitful—hover behind *Little Gidding's* action as approach to dying. Varied means lead to the same end, block (or scaffold), fire, drowning (reviewing the allusions in *Little Gidding* to the execution of the "broken king" and to the incendiary raids on war-stricken London, and in *The Dry Salvages* to death by water) or natural death and sleep in the country churchyard (the "illegible stones" we have met before as "Old stones that cannot be deciphered" [EC 198]). Once more end is beginning, for "that is where we start" (229). For four lines (230-233) the cycle of end and beginning, death and rebirth, departure and return is the subject of gentle iteration. Line shape and phrasing help for "We die...," "See, they depart..." are closely mirrored in "We are born...," "See, they return...."

"The moment of the rose" (234) as that of *Burnt Norton's* garden experience is characterized by intensity and timelessness; the correlative "moment of the yew-tree," symbol of immortality, is timeless in another sense. For both, "duration" (235) is swallowed up in eternity. Eliot's strong sense of tradition is felt behind the plea for history, his love of "ordonnance" in the insistence on "pattern."[17] "Pattern," "stillness," "timeless moments" are verbal approaches to the ineffable in supra-mundane contacts and to that which gives meaning to the stretches of life between.

The "winter's afternoon" (238) at the end of the journey to the shrine sounds the same as that at the beginning (8); that was characterized as "early," while now "the light fails" (237), a circumstance possibly significant of more than the advancing hour. The role of "light" has shifted somewhat from *Quartet* to *Quartet*.[18] In *Burnt Norton* it was associated with clarity and life; in *East Coker* it seemed elusive and not altogether wholesome; *The Dry Salvages* dispenses with it entirely; in *Little Gidding* its sole appearance is in this line. The darkness of this "secluded chapel" (238)[19] shall frame the moment of "valid" prayer and deep communion, and "tongued with fire" (53) shall illuminate the troubled land and era from its ardent source in the devout community and the latter's moving spirit, bridging time by shared experience and fruitful contemplation whose motive force is as with the author of *The Cloud of Unknowing* "the drawing of this Love and the voice of this Calling" (240).

241 [20]We shall not cease from exploration
242 And the end of all our exploring
243 Will be to arrive where we started
244 And know the place for the first time.
245 Through the unknown, remembered gate
246 When the last of earth left to discover
247 Is that which was the beginning;
248 At the source of the longest river
249 The voice of the hidden waterfall
250 And the children in the apple-tree
251 Not known, because not looked for
252 But heard, half-heard, in the stillness
253 Between two waves of the sea.
254 Quick now, here, now, always—
255 A condition of complete simplicity
256 (Costing not less than everything)
257 And all shall be well and
258 All manner of thing shall be well
259 When the tongues of flame are in-folded
260 Into the crowned knot of fire
261 And the fire and the rose are one.

Remembering that "Old men ought to be explorers" (*EC* 199) "We shall not cease from exploration" (241). The searching mind has in the course of the *Quartets* spiralled round the heart of the matter, coming always a little closer to expression of what the seeker knows intuitively of the soul's center and its dealings there with God and creatures. With arrival at the starting point ("In my end is my beginning") the purified vision admits a new knowledge, or rather an understanding, of what was imperfectly, however, tenaciously, grasped at the gate of the early garden, be it a personal Eden of innocence or (more appropriately to the overall context) a season of realization of identity and relation unmatched in acuity but so far defying re-presentation save through the distortion of time. Time transcended and stillness attained, the past and its symbols are present realities—so the river and the waterfall and the children and the sea and the bidding bird—in the "condition of complete simplicity" (255) at the cost of complete detachment[21] and all is well. The tongues of fire that taught and chastened have returned whence they issued and the heart of the rose of light (*Paradiso* XXXI) is the vision vouchsafed the seeker.

Conclusion

A FEW GENERAL principles may be derived from the foregoing pages. The first and most obvious is that everything counts. The second, hardly less obvious, is that everything is related. And on these two depends the entire elaborate reticulation demanding undistracted attention of eye and ear and memory while the imagination is spurred to multiply associations and mix its own sauces. Nor is the intellect idle; its task is "the intolerable wrestle with words and meanings" (*EC* 71-72).

From the word outward Eliot savors every saying. Words in combination are patterned for their sound and lettering, line position, weight and tempo, force as echo, semantic synonymity or contrast as well as for their strict syntactic functions and relations. The building of the sense units (for the most part grammatically regular) calls into play such non-syntactic features as elements contributing to broader tonal effects and desired emphases. These devices are to the sentence as the player's gestures and facial expression to his spoken part. In some few instances (notably *Burnt Norton* I) they have a logic of their own which counterpoints the surface meaning and suggests underlying tensions. Elsewhere they intensify by positive support the tenor of the discourse and the definite mood evoked. Eliot's rhetoric therefore complements his syntax and deals in matters beyond the latter's scope.

His diction may be said to meet his own exacting standards (see *Little Gidding* V). Rich and varied certainly, true at every elevation of pitch, shown to advantage in any prosodic setting, his words are chosen with reference to this basic rule: "Poetry must not stray too far from the ordinary everyday language which we use and hear. Whether poetry is accentual or syllabic, rhymed or rhymeless, formal or free, it cannot afford to lose its contact with the changing language of common intercourse."[1]

Speaking of Eliot's example as of the greatest help to young poets in transitional rather than climactic passages a critic observes that "they reveal to him the possibility of conveying in verse, with exactness, an equivalent of his passing moods and of the tone, and even of the shades of tone, of his individual speaking voice."[2]

This is of course quite in keeping with Eliot's insistence that

> it would be a mistake ... to assume that all poetry ought to be melodious, or that melody is more than one of the components of the music of words .... Dissonance, even cacophony, has its place: just as in a poem of any length, there must be transitions between passages of greater and less intensity, to give a rhythm of fluctuating emotion essential to the musical structure of the whole; and the passages of less intensity will be, in relation to the level on which the total poem operates, prosaic—so that, in the sense implied by that context, it may be said that no poet can write a poem of amplitude unless he is a master of the prosaic.

> This is the complementary doctrine to that of the 'touchstone' line or passage of Matthew Arnold: this test of the greatness of a poet is the way he writes his less intense, but structurally vital, matter.[3]

In this connection we notice that the large proportion of conjunctions, prepositions, relatives and demonstratives in the *Quartet* vocabulary does not make for dilution of the poetically significant, but is doubly useful in binding it within a framework of comprehensibility and in providing a manipulable setting for the basic material of his evocative or incantatory phrase-making. (He censures as "tiring to the eye and ear" the "monotonously short lines with excess of stops and defect of connectives"[4] of some of Hilda Doolittle's classical translations.)

Perhaps the strongest evidence of Eliot's mastery of language is the extraordinary power he communicates to a word or phrase by virtue merely of his using it a second time. Each repetition brings its increment of meaning and sets up vibrations as it were which waken a complex response and still more a feeling that more is said than can be fully taken in, and that it will keep on ringing in the consciousness. A not very dignified comparison suggests itself in the nerve net of the hydra (not the mythical monster but its diminutive namesake) whose response to a given stimulus is not localized but of the whole organism.

The vitality of the poem confronts us on every human level. Yet its words reshuffled would offer little by way of distinctive clue to their force in Eliot's ranks. Its syntactical structure though now and then appalling would in the main delight the grammarian whose sentence diagrams could branch like fir-trees. The rhetorician, mediaeval or modern, could line his handbook with examples culled from one who learned well of his masters.

This vitality is the principle of the formal organization of the poem which Eliot tells us "comes before the form, in the sense that a form grows out of the attempt of somebody to say something; just as a system of prosody is only a formulation of the identities in the rhythms of a succession of poets influenced by each other."[5]

An early pronouncement of Eliot's made in wry answer to a questionnaire (his amusedly tolerant reception of a similar query has already been noted, see note 14 to Chapter 3, below) submitted by Harold Monro to twenty-seven individuals proves seriously prophetic of his own achievement. To the three questions:

1. Do you think that poetry is a necessity to modern man?
2. What in modern life is the particular function of poetry as distinguished from other kinds of literature?
3. Do you think there is any chance of verse being eventually displaced by prose, as narrative poetry apparently is being by the novel, and ballads already have been by newspaper reports?

Eliot's replies, by far the briefest of those published were:

1.   No.
2.   Takes up less space.
3.   It is up to the poets to find something to do in verse which cannot be done in any other form.[6]

Four Quartets meets the challenge. And it is as form that it chiefly satisfies the need it recognizes in its persistent quest for "pattern." The ubiquity and significance of pattern in the *Quartets* leads to a final conclusion that it is intrinsic and functional and nowhere merely decorative. The rhetoric issues from the deeper matrix of feeling as the syntax reflects the windings of thought and the diction proceeds from irrefrangible contact with reality.

NOTES

Introduction

[1] "A Commentary: That Poetry is made with Words," *New English Weekly*, XV (Apr. 27, 1939), 27.

[2] The edition used is that of *Complete Poems and Plays* (New York, 1952). Minor typographical discrepancies between this and the separate editons of *Four Quartets* (New York, 1943 [Harcourt Brace] and London, 1944 [Faber]) are noted as they occur.

[3] "Observations," *Egoist*, V (1918), 69. (Signed "T. S. Apteryx")

[4] "The Writer as Artist: Discussion between T. S. Eliot and Desmond Hawkins," *Listener*, XXIV (Nov. 28, 1940), 774.

[5] "The Aims of Education. 1. Can 'Education' be Defined?" *Measure*, II (1950), 14. See also "The Social Function of Poetry," *Norseman*, I (1943), 449-457 (reprinted with slight modifications in *Adelphi*, XXI [1945], 152-161; this version is also reprinted in Robert Wooster Stallman, ed., *Critiques and Essays in Criticism* [New York, 1949], pp. 106-16) and "The Responsibility of the Man of Letters in the Cultural Restoration of Europe," *Norseman*, II (1944), 243-48.

[6] "John Maynard Keynes," *NEW*, XXIX (May 16, 1946), 48.

[7] "From Poe to Valéry," *Hudson Review*, II (1949), 333.

[8] *Ibid.*, 332.

[9] *Times Literary Supplement*, No. 1337 (Sept. 15, 1927), 620. (Donald Gallup, *T. S. Eliot: a Bibliography* [New York, 1953], p. 93, annotates this entry, a review of L. C. Martin's edition of Crashaw, as somewhat doubtfully of Eliot's authorship.)

[10] "The Poetry of W. B. Yeats," *Southern Review*, VII (1942), 451.

[11] "Prose and Verse," *Chapbook*, No. 22 (April 1921). 8.

[12] *Selected Essays* (New York, 1932) (hereafter referred to as *SE*) alone is sufficient to document the enumerated qualities: immediacy and particularity, pp. 183, 185; compression, pp. 48, 200; austerity, p. 213; lucidity, p. 201; aptness, pp. 130, 169, 295.

[13] See especially Eliot's remarks on Swinburne's uprooted and atmospherically nourished language (*SE*, p. 283) as well as the familiar strictures regarding the "dissociation of sensibility" (*SE*, p. 185).

[14] "Prose and Verse," *Chapbook*, No. 22 (April 1921), 5.

[15] See p. 128.

16 "A Commentary: That Poetry is made with Words," *NEW*, XV (Apr. 27, 1939), 27. See also *The Music of Poetry* [pamphlet]...the third W. P. Ker Memorial Lecture delivered in the University of Glasgow, 24th February, 1942 (G. U. P. LVII) (Glasgow, 1942), p. 9.

17 But see Joseph Frank, "Spatial Form in Modern Literature" in Stallman, *Critiques*, pp. 315-328.

18 *SE*, p. 8.

19 "In Praise of Kipling's Verse," *Harper's*, CLXXXV (1942), 152. See also *Music of Poetry*, p. 13: "The music of poetry is not something which exists apart from the meaning."

20 "Marianne Moore" [A review of *Poems* and *Marriage*], *Dial*, LXXV (1923), 595. Eliot selects "Those Various Scalpels" as "an excellent example for study. Here the rhythm depends partly upon the transformation-change from one image to another, so that the second image is superposed before the first has quite faded, and upon the dexterity of change of vocabulary from one image to another."

21 Sept. 13, 1928.

22 *TLS*, 1391 (Sept. 27, 1928), 687.

23 See, e.g., BN 46, 54ff.; EC 130-134; DS 77, 213; LG 10.

24 *Dial*, LXXV (1923), 595.

25 *Harper's*, CLXXXV (1942), 150.

26 *Ibid.*, 152.

27 *The Art of T. S. Eliot* (New York, 1950) and "Four Quartets: a Commentary" in Stallman, ed., *Critiques*, pp. 181-197. Miss Gardner after noting that "each poem is structurally a poetic equivalent of the classical symphony, or quartet, or sonata, as distinct from the suite" (*Art*, pp. 36-37) goes on to show how the five "movements" in each *Quartet* are constructed on musical principles and may without violence be described in terms of manipulation of musical themes. (*Ibid.*, pp. 37-42.)

28 "A Note on the Verse of John Milton," *Essays and Studies by Members of the English Association*, XXI (1935), 33.

29 *Art of T. S. Eliot*, ch. I, "Auditory Imagination," especially pp. 3-6.

30 Edward J. H. Greene, *T. S. Eliot et la France*, Etudes de littérature étrangère et comparée (Paris, [1951]), p. 92.

31 Ezra Pound, "Drunken Helots and Mr. Eliot," *Egoist*, IV (1917), 75.

32 "Sir John Denham," *TLS*, No. 1379 (July 5, 1928), 501.

33 "Prose and Verse," *Chapbook*, No. 22 (April 1921), 9.

34 *Ibid.*, 3. We are warned elsewhere of the fallacy of the "conversational style"—"an *identical* spoken and written language would be practically intolerable." (*SE*, p. 407.)

35 "Rhetoric and Poetic Drama" in *SE*, p. 26.

36 *Ibid.*, pp. 25, 26.

37 *SE*, p. 245.

38 "The development of technique is a serious and unceasing subject of study among verse writers...." (*Criterion*, IX [1930], 588.)

39 See, in their proper places, the many phrasal echoes from earlier poems (or plays).

40 *Music of Poetry*, p. 25.

41 *Ibid.*, p. 8.

42 *Criterion*, XV (1936), 708.

Chapter 1
Burnt Norton

1 The edition quoted throughout is that of *Complete Poems and Plays*. Discrepancies between this and the Faber edition of *Four Quartets* (London, 1944) will be noted as they occur.

2 We are indebted to Raymond Preston, *Four Quartets Rehearsed* (New York, 1946), for pointing out the interesting parallel with Ecclesiastes iii, 15: "That which hath been is now; and that which is to be hath already been; and God requireth that which is past."

3 See below, pp. 46-47, 53.

4 *Music of Poetry*, p. 14. See also "A Note on Poetry and Belief," *Enemy*, I (1927) 15: "I do not believe that an author is more qualified to elucidate the esoteric significance of his own work, than is any other person of training and sensibility and at least equal intelligence."

5 "Vergil and the Christian World," *Listener*, XLVI (1951), 411.

6 p. 2.

7 (Chicago, 1950), I, 197-219.

8 Cf. *The Family Reunion*, Part II, Scene iii (*CPP*, p. 277) and *The Confidential Clerk*, Act II (New York: Harcourt Brace, 1954), pp. 63-66.

9 Preston comments on their signification: "The juxtaposition of the dead rose-leaves and the living rose-garden effected by these lines which introduce the vision is characteristic: a way of luring the reader to see and to feel and at the same time maintaining a detachment from nostaligic indulgence. It conveys the doubt and hesitation of the opening in imagery." (*Four Quartets Rehearsed*, p. 13.)
    Pertinent to the portion dealt with so far is a remark of B. H. Fussell who cites intellectual analysis and emotional immediacy, logical abstraction and concrete metaphor as "Structural Methods in *Four Quartets*" (*ELH*, XXII [1955], 212-241): "What is new to Eliot's own development is his use of a deliberately heightened 'dissociation of sensibility.'". (p. 213).

10 See above, p. x.

11 See, e.g., the garden in *Ash-Wednesday* II (*CPP*, p. 62), the hermit-thrush in *The Waste Land* V (*CPP*, p. 48), Kipling's *They* and Grimm's *Juniper Tree*.

12 We can leave to the ornithologists the literalistic reading which sees in this word a reference to the habit of the water-thrush of dragging its wing along the ground, pretending injury, to lead an interloper away from its nest. (Mark Reinsberg, "A Footnote to *Four Quartets*," *American Literature*, XXI [1949], 343.)

13 See *The Waste Land*, 11. 220-222 (*CPP*, pp. 43-44):
   ...the evening hour that strives
   Homeward, and brings...
   The typist home at teatime, clears her breakfast,
                                              . . .

14 The rhetorical structure, as it is hoped will be shown, argues against reading the second "they" as standing for the roses just described and seeing as the reflection in the pool only the formal flower beds. (Incidentally, the pool had no water in it to reflect what was really there, and, besides, seems to have been bordered by the "box circle.")

15 Here is the same transcendence of the ordinary noted above (p. 2) in a kind of implied oxymoron.

16 As Preston interprets the passage, *op. cit.*, p. 13.

17 The second can in this connection be extended four more lines to include 45.

18 See above, p. 8.

19 See, e.g., *Gerontion* (*CPP*, p. 21): "The word within a word, unable to speak a word," a line taken from a sermon by Lancelot Andrewes. See *SE*, pp. 331-343, for eloquent testimony to Eliot's admiration for this seventeenth century figure.

20 See above, p. x.

21 There is no indentation in this and similar passages in the Faber or Harcourt Brace editions of the *Four Quartets* in separate book form.

22 For this insight we are indebted to Dr. Charles Donahue of Fordham University.

23 [Alexis Saint-Léger], *Anabasis: a poem* by St.-John Perse translated by T. S. Eliot (New York, 1949), p. 11.

24 But the punctuation, the solitary comma which serves only to separate subject from predicate, is dictated by desire for speech pause rather than grammatical clarity.

25 See above, p. x.

26 Hugh Kenner notes: "The realization of images only so much as is needful is a major rhetorical device through the *Quartets*." ("Eliot's Moral Dialectic," *Hudson Review* II [1949], 434-435.)

27 *CPP*, p. 38.

28 Or does the rose-garden represent imaginary past; the arbor, real past; the church, future? (Dr. Charles Donahue)

29 Webster's example is, strikingly, "the *affections* of time and place."

30 In Eliot's pronunciation, the word assonates with "light."

31 Notably by Leonard Unger, "T. S. Eliot's Rose Garden" in *T. S. Eliot: a Selected Critique* (New York, 1948), p. 383.

32 Helen Gardner so identifies the setting, *The Art of T. S. Eliot* (New York, 1950), p. 161.

33 See also D. S. Bland's comments on the "Inner Circle" of the London underground system apropos of its specific mention in *East Coker*, p. 60.

34 See also *Little Gidding* 89.

35 Thoreau notes: "April 24, 1854. The kingfisher flies with a *crack cr-r-r-ack* and a limping or flitting flight from tree to tree before us, and finally, after a third of a mile, circles round to our rear." (*Thoreau's Bird-lore*, ed. Francis H. Allen [Boston, 1925], p. 192.)

36 *The Oxford Dictionary* notwithstanding, the main stress on "Chinese" as used in this line falls on the first syllable. This need not be a surviving Americanism on Eliot's part; it has been spontaneously so read, without exception, by several available British accents.

37 Neither this nor "lasts" in 147 would be flat to Eliot or his British readers.

38 These might include the simultaneity of "perspective" in which all distance, like all time, is "eternally present;" the essentially symbolic character of Chinese portraiture and abstract design (see Helen Gardner, *Art Through the Ages* [New York, 1948], pp. 378-385); the disposition of color to secure maximum effect of light and contour.

Chapter 2
East Coker

1 See especially: James Johnson Sweeney, "East Coker: a Reading," *Southern Review*, VI (1941), 771-791; Curtis Bradford, "Footnotes to East Coker: a Reading," *Sewanee Review*, 52 (1944), 169-175; Francis J. Smith, "A Reading of East Coker," *Thought*, XXI (1946), 272-286; also Preston and Gardner.

2 We are reminded that *East Coker* was written for Good Friday, 1940. (Preston, p. 34n.)

3 Joseph Beaver, "T. S. Eliot's *Four Quartets*," *Explicator*, XI (1953), 37.

4 The word "grimpen" is not given in *OED* or in any of several dialect dictionaries consulted. Eliot's use has been traced only to

Conan Doyle's *Hound of the Baskervilles* (see James Johnson Sweeney, "East Coker: a Reading," *Southern Review,* VI (1941), 780). It is suggested that the term may be a corruption of a place name; Grampound, a village in Cornwall on the Fal River, seems a plausible candidate. Climactic and geographical features point to a marshy terrain, and the westward extension of the locale of the poem is of advantage in providing celebrated 6th and 7thC sepulchre inscriptions for the "old stones that cannot be deciphered" (198), while geological evidence of (prehistoric) sinking of the land in this quarter joins remembered changes in the profile of the Cornish coast to lend credence to the literalistic reading of "The houses are all gone under the sea" (100) tentatively put forward below, note 6.

5 In *CPP.* In the separate Harcourt Brace edition of *Four Quartets* (1943), the lines are spaced but not indented.

6 If it is not irrelevant and trivial to press for literal justification here, coastal erosion might account for the submarine fate, but tonally we are closer to Prufrock's sea chambers than to the geologist's study. Similarly, if "hill" be questioned we remember that the "deep lane" beside the field had a bank high enough to "lean against...while a van passes." Thus the field can conveniently be converted into a plateau. But the proximity of a hill may be safely assumed from the necessity of housing the wee folk who traditionally lived in hills.

7 See, e.g., *CPP,* pp. 3, 41, 43, 46, 47, 65, 72, 89, 105, although these occurrences include the conversational "oh" and the "o" of scriptural quotation or ritual intent.

8 See above, p. 24.

9 See above, pp. 3-4.

10 D. S. Bland, "Mr. Eliot on the Underground," *MLN,* LXVIII (1953), 27-28.

11 See, e.g., *BN,* 4-5 (above, p. 4); *EC,* 10-11, 12-13, 52-53, 54-56 (above, p. 49), 79-82 (above, p. 52).

12 *Complete Poems of Robert Frost: 1949* (New York, 1949), p. 53.

13 There is no indentation before this and the following stanzas in the separate edition of *Four Quartets* (1943).

14 See, e.g., the studies noted above in note 1 of this chapter.

Chapter 3
The Dry Salvages

1 This is true even of "frontier" (3) according to the *Concise Oxford Dictionary.*

2 *CPP,* p. 37.

3 "There is...one error in the text [of *Four Quartets*] which has

escaped the observaton of any of my friends or critics, and of which I have only just myself [sic] become aware. In the first section of 'The Dry Salvages,' 'the hermit crab' should be 'horse-shoe crab.' It was, of course, the horse-shoe crab that I had in mind: the slip must have been due to the fact that I did not want a spondee in that place. What is more curious is that the term 'hermit crab' should have continued to do duty for 'horse-shoe crab' in my mind, in this context, from the date of original publication [Feb. 27, 1941 (NEW)] until last week. I shall be grateful to any of your readers who may possess the poem, if they will kindly make the alteration." (Letter to the Editor, NEW, XXVI [Jan. 25, 1945], 112.)

4 See especially CPP, pp. 207-209.

5 Interesting in this connection, mutatis mutandis, is a remark of Eliot's calling "attention to a trick of Seneca of repeating one word of a phrase in the next phrase...where the sentence of one speaker is caught up and twisted by the next. This was an effective stage trick, but it is something more; it is the crossing of one rhythm pattern with another." (SE, p. 72)

6 There is no indentation at this or the following stanza heads in the separate edition of Four Quartets (1943).

7 (N.Y., 1951), pp. 58, 70ff.

8 See especially CPP, pp. 275-277 (Harry and Agatha); p. 251 (Harry and Mary) is also interesting for its bearing on the themes of the sestina.

9 See above, pp. 69-70.

10 See above, p. 61.

11 CPP, p. 46.

12 See especially: "Ye shall pray also for all who travel by land, sea, or air; for all prisoners and captives; for all who are in sickness or in sorrow; for all who have fallen into grievous sin; for all who, through temptation, ignorance, helplessness, grief, trouble, dread, or the near approach of death, especially need our prayers." (Seabury Press, Greenwich, Conn., 1953, p. 48).

13 There is no indentation before these stanzas in the separate edition of Four Quartets.

14 An interesting prose verification of this attitude is Eliot's courteous but unambiguous reply to Eugene Jolas' questionnaire, "Inquiry into the Spirit and Language of Night," which asked a number of writers: "1. What was your most recent characteristic dream (or day-dream, waking-sleeping hallucination, phantasma)? 2. Have you observed any ancestral myths or symbols in your collective unconscious? 3. Have you ever felt the need for a new language to express the experiences of your night mind?" Eliot answered: "I am afraid I cannot be of much use to you with your questionnaire. Questions number 1 and 2 are really matters I prefer

to keep to myself. The answer to number 3 is definitely *no.* I am not, as a matter of fact, particularly interested in my 'night-mind.' This is not a general assertion about night-minds, nor does it carry any suggestion about other people's interest in their night-minds. It is only that I find my own quite uninteresting." (*Transition*, No. 27 [Apr./May 1938], 233, 236.

15 "The Pope and the UN," *Integrity*, Jan., 1956, p. 11.

16 Dom Aelred Watkin, *The Heart of the World* (New York, 1954), p. 21.

17 *Ibid.*, p. 14.

18 *Ibid.*, pp. 21-22.

19 The period which closes this line in *CPP* is obviously a misprint and is therefore omitted here. There is none in the Faber (1944) or Harcourt Brace (1943) separate editions of *Four Quartets,* nor in *The Dry Salvages* as published in *NEW*, XVIII (Feb. 27, 1941), 220. That textual variants may some day be a problem in Eliot studies is attested to by William H. Marshall ("The Text of T. S. Eliot's 'Gerontion'," *Studies in Bibliography*, IV (1951-1952), 213-217) who lists the variants in *Gerontion* as printed in seven collected editions, with final approval by Eliot of the version chosen for a University of Virginia McGregor Room Seminar program. Eliot's alterations favored different editions in the several instances of discrepancies in punctuation or a word here and there.

20 See above, pp. 26-27.

Chapter 4
Little Gidding

1 Miles Hadfield, *An English Almanac* (London, 1950), p. 16.

2 Joseph Beaver, *Explicator*, XI (1953), no. 37.

3 See note 5 to Chapter 3, above.

4 *CPP*, p. 176.

5 *Ibid.*, p. 201.

6 *Ibid.*, p. 184.

7 *Ibid.*, p. 221.

8 See above, pp. 63-64.

9 *CPP*, p. 221.

10 This is the same in all editions consulted.

11 By a trick of association—and association with Shakespeare's "bare, ruin'd choirs" (Sonnet LXXIII) is immediate—we go from "where late the sweet birds sang" to the insistent bird of *Burnt Norton*'s garden, and the cycle of the *Quartets* is complete in this third stanza.

12 Before leaving this stanza it might be instructive to look at some

of Eliot's other roses—*Ash Wednesday*'s "Rose of memory / Rose of forgetfulness" (*CPP*, p. 62) comes to mind at once; especially interesting in the present connection are two lines omitted in *CPP* as in the first separate edition (London, 1930) but included in the earlier version of Part II which appeared as *Salutation* in *Saturday Review of Literature*, IV (Dec. 10, 1927), 429, and in *Criterion*, VII (Jan. 1928), 31-32. The *Criterion* version is as follows:

> End of the endless
> Journey to no end
> Conclusion of all that
> Is inconclusible
> Speech without word and
> Word of no speech
> Grace to the Mother
> * For the end of remembering
> * End of forgetting
> For the Garden
> Where all love ends   (p. 32)

(*indicates lines omitted in *CPP*; there are other such omissions as well as alterations in punctuation and an occasional word—those concerning the Rose [also in the "Lady of silences" passage] are "Spattered and worshipped" deleted after "Rose of forgetfulness" and "With worm eaten petals" deleted after "The single Rose.")

Perhaps coincidence but certainly arresting in connection with "burnt roses" is the occurrence in Francis Thompson's *Mistress of Vision*—also set in a garden, also referring to Our Lady—of the lines:

> ...as a necromancer
> Raises from the rose-ash
> The ghost of the rose;
> > (*Complete Poetical Works*
> > [New York (1913)], p. 185.)

13 *CPP*, p. 21.

14 *Ibid.*, p. 39.

15 See above, Introduction, p. i. For Pound's views, see, e.g., *How to Read* (Le Beausset, Var., France* [1932], pp. 14-15; *Instigations* (New York, 1920), pp. 109-111; *Spirit of Romance* (London, 1910), p. vii; *The Letters of Ezra Pound*, ed. D. D. Paige (New York, 1950), pp. 8-9.

*The Library of Congress catalogue gives for this edition: "Imprint under label: Boston, Bruce Humphries [1932]"

16 The Faber (1944) *Four Quartets* leaves an additional space between 239 and 240. These lines are on different pages in the Harcourt Brace edition (1943) so the intention cannot be determined.

17 This is the tenth occurrence of the word in *Four Quartets*.

18 See concordance.

19 See also "The moment in the draughty church at smokefall" (*BN* 90).

[20] There is no indentation here in the separate editions.

[21] It is a detachment, however, which integrates, on a higher plane, that from which one is detached. The last lines can mean simply that all shall be well in heaven, where the Church Triumphant (the "rose") is united in and with the Holy Ghost (the "fire"). The timeless moments of this life, whether aesthetic (*Burnt Norton*), ethical (*The Dry Salvages*), or religious (*Little Gidding*) are analogues, "intimations," of the final state of the blessed. We are indebted for this insight to Dr. Charles Donahue of Fordham University.

Conclusion

[1] *Music of Poetry*, p. 13.

[2] G. S. Fraser, "A Language by Itself" in Richard March and Tambimuttu, compilers, *T. S. Eliot: a Symposium* (Chicago, 1949), p. 170.

[3] *Music of Poetry*, pp. 17-18.

[4] "Classics in English," *Poetry*, IX, 2 (Nov. 1916), 103.

[5] *Music of Poetry*, p. 26.

[6] "Answers to the Three Questions," *Chapbook*, No. 27 (July, 1922), 8.

BIBLIOGRAPHY

Beaver, Joseph. "T. S. Eliot's *Four Quartets*," *Explicator*, XI (1953), No. 37.

Bland, D. S. "Mr. Eliot on the Underground," *MLN*, LXVIII (1953), 27-28.

Book of Common Prayer. Greenwich, Conn.: The Seabury Press, 1953.

Bradford, Curtis. "Footnotes to East Coker: a Reading," *Sewanee Review*, LII (1944), 169-175.

Carson, Rachel. *The Sea Around Us*. New York: Oxford University Press, 1951.

Daiches, David. *Poetry and the Modern World*. Chicago: University of Chicago Press, 1941.

————. "Some Aspects of T. S. Eliot," *College English*, IX (1947), 115-122.

Eliot, Thomas Stearns. "The Aims of Education. 1. Can 'Education' be Defined?" *Measure*, II, (1950), [3]-16.

————. *American Literature and the American Language*. Washington University Studies, New Series, Language and Literature, No. 23. St. Louis: Washington University, 1953.

————. "Answers to the Three Questions," *Chapbook*, No. 27 (July, 1922), 8.

————. *The Classics and the Man of Letters* London: Oxford University Press, 1942.

————. "Classics in English," *Poetry*, IX (1916), 101-104.

————. "A Commentary: the Teaching of English," *Criterion*, VI (1927), 289-291.

————. "A Commentary: the Dean's English," *Criterion*, VI (1927), 481-483.

————. "A Commentary," *Criterion*. IX (1930), 587-590.

————. "A Commentary," *Criterion*, XI (1932), 676-683.

————. "A Commentary," *Criterion*, XII (1933), 244-249.

————. "A Commentary," *Criterion*, XIV (1935), 610-613.

————. "A Commentary: That Poetry is Made with Words," *New English Weekly*, XV (1939), 27-28.

————. *Complete Poems and Plays*. New York: Harcourt, Brace, 1952.

————. *The Confidential Clerk*. New York: Harcourt Brace, 1954.

————. "Crashaw's Poetical Works," *Times Literary Supplement*, No. 1337 (Sept. 15, 1927), 620.

————. *Four Quartets.* New York: Harcourt Brace, [1943].

————. *Four Quartets.* London: Faber and Faber [1944].

————. "From Poe to Valéry," *Hudson Review*, II (1949), [327]-342.

————. "Grammar and Usage," *Criterion*, V (1927), 121-124.

————. "The Idea of a Literary Review," *Criterion*, IV (1926), 1-6.

————. "In Praise of Kipling's Verse," *Harper's* CLXXXV (1942), [149]-157.

————. "John Maynard Keynes," *New English Weekly*, XXIX (1946), 47-48.

————. "The 'Four Quartets'" [A Letter to the Editor], *New English Weekly*, XXVI (1945), 112.

————. "Marianne Moore," *Dial*, LXXV (1923), [594]-597.

————. *Milton.* London: Geoffrey Cumberlege. 1948.

————. "Mr. Lucas's Webster," *Criterion*, VII (1928), 155-158.

————. "Mr. Murray's Shakespeare," *Criterion*, XV (1936), 708-710.

————. *The Music of Poetry,* Glasgow University Publications, No. 57. Glasgow: Jackson, 1942.

————. "The Need for Poetic Drama," *Listener*, XVI (1936), 994-995.

————. "A Note on Poetry and Belief," *Enemy*, I (1927), 15-17.

————. "Note sur Mallarmé et Poe," transl. Ramon Fernandez [English text not published], *Nouvelle Revue Française*, XIV (1926), 524-526.

————. "A Note on the Verse of John Milton," *Essays and Studies*, XXI (1935), 32-41.

————. "Observations," *Egoist*, V (1918), 69-70 [signed "T. S. Apteryx"].

————. "The Poetry of W. B. Yeats," *Southern Review*, VII (1941), 442-454.

————. "Prose and Verse," *Chapbook*, No. 22 (April, 1921), 3-10.

————. "Questions of Prose" [A Letter to the Editor], *Times Literary Supplement*, No. 1391 (Sept. 27, 1928), 687.

————. "The Responsibility of the Man of Letters in the Cultural Restoration of Europe," *Norseman*, II (1944), 243-248.

————. "Salutation," *Criterion*, VII (1928), 31-32.

————. *Selected Essays 1917-1932,* New York: Harcourt, Brace, 1932.

————. "Sir John Denham," *Times Literary Supplement*, No. 1379 (July 5, 1928), 501.

————. "The Social Function of Poetry," *Norseman*, I (1943), 449-457.

————. "Vergil and the Christian World," *Listener*, XLVI (1951), 411-412, 423-424.

————. "The Writer as Artist: Discussion between T. S. Eliot and Desmond Hawkins," *Listener*, XXIV (1940), 773-774.

Frank, Joseph. "Spatial Form in Modern Literature" in *Critiques and Essays in Criticism 1920-1948*, ed. Robert Wooster Stallman. New York: Ronald Press, 1949. pp. 315-328.

Fraser, George Sutherland. "A Language by Itself" in *T. S. Eliot: a Symposium*, compiled by Richard March and Tambimuttu. Chicago: Regnery, 1949. pp. 167-177.

Fussell, B. H. "Structural Methods in *Four Quartets*," *ELH* XXII (1955), 212-241.

Gallup, Donald Clifford. *T. S. Eliot: a Bibliography*. New York: Harcourt, Brace, 1953.

Gardner, Helen. *Art Through the Ages*. New York: Harcourt, Brace, 1942.

Gardner, Helen L[ouise]. *The Art of T. S. Eliot*. New York: Dutton, 1950.

————. "Four Quartets: a Commentary" in *Critiques and Essays in Criticism*, pp. 181-197. [See Frank, Joseph, above.]

Greene, Edward J[oseph] H[allingsworth]. *T. S. Eliot et la France*. Paris: Boivin, [1951].

Hadfield, Miles. *An English Almanac*. London: Dent, 1950.

Hamilton, G[eorge] Rostrevor. *The Tell-Tale Article: a Critical Approach to Modern Poetry*. New York: Oxford University Press, 1950.

Jolas, Eugene. "Inquiry into the Spirit and Language of Night," *Transition*, No. 27 (April-May, 1938), 233-236.

Kenner, Hugh. "Eliot's Moral dialectic," *Hudson Review*, II (1949), 421-448.

Leavis, Frank Raymond. *New Bearings in English Poetry*. New York: George W. Stewart, 1950.

[Léger, Alexis Saint-Léger]. *Anabasis*: a poem by St.-John Perse translated by T. S. Eliot. New York: Harcourt, Brace, 1949.

Marcel, Gabriel. *Mystery of Being*, I. Chicago: Regnery, 1950.

Marshall, William H. "The Text of T. S. Eliot's 'Gerontion'," *Studies in Bibliography*, IV (1951-1952), 213-217.

Matthiessen, Francis Otto. *The Achievement of T. S. Eliot*. 2nd edition. New York: Oxford University Press, 1947.

Muir, Edwin. A review of *After Strange Gods*, (London) *Spectator*, CLII (1934), 378-579.

————. A review of *Collected Poems*, (London) *Spectator*, CLVI (1936), 622.

Musgrove, S. *T. S. Eliot and Walt Whitman*. Wellington, New Zealand: New Zealand University Press, 1952.

Pound, Ezra. "Drunken Helots and Mr. Eliot," *Egoist*, IV (1917), 75.

————. *How to Read.* Boston: Bruce Humphries, [1932].

————. *Instigations.* New York: Boni and Liveright, [1920].

————. *The Letters of Ezra Pound,* ed. D. D. Paige. New York: Harcourt, Brace, [1950].

————. A review of *Prufrock and Other Observations, Poetry,* X (1917), 264-271.

————. *The Spirit of Romance,* London: Dent, [1910].

Praz, Mario. "T. S. Eliot and Dante," *Southern Review,* II (1937), 525-548.

Preston, Raymond. *'Four Quartets' Rehearsed.* New York: Sheed and Ward, 1946.

Quinn, Sister Mary Bernetta. *The Metamorphic Tradition in Modern Poetry.* New Brunswick, N. J.: Rutgers University Press, 1955.

Rajan, Balachandra. "The Unity of the *Quartets*" in *T. S. Eliot: a Study of His Writings by Several Hands,* ed. B. Rajan, New York: Funk and Wagnalls, 1949. pp. 78-95.

Reinsberg, Mark. "A Footnote to Four Quartets," *American Literature,* XX (1949), 343.

Smith, Francis J. "A Reading of East Coker," *Thought,* XX (1946), 272-286.

Sweeney, James Johnson. "East Coker: a Reading," *Southern Review,* VI (1941), 771-791.

Thompson, Francis. *Complete Poetical Works.* New York: Boni and Liveright, [1913].

Thoreau's Bird-Lore, ed. Francis H. Allen. Boston: Houghton Mifflin, 1925.

Tindall, William York. *The Literary Symbol.* New York: Columbia University Press, 1955.

Wagner, Robert D. "The Meaning of Eliot's Rose-Garden," *PMLA,* LXIX (1954), 22-33.

Watkin, Dom Aelred. *The Heart of the World.* New York: Kenedy, 1954.

Williams, Charles. *All Hallows' Eve,* with introduction by T. S. Eliot. New York: Pellegrini and Cudahy, [1948].

Williams, Raymond. *Drama from Ibsen to Eliot.* New York: Oxford University Press, 1953.

Williamson, George. *A Reader's Guide to T. S. Eliot.* New York: Noonday Press, 1953.

Wilson, Frank. *Six Essays on the Development of T. S. Eliot.* London: Fortune Press, 1948.

Unger, Leonard. "T. S. Eliot's Rose Garden" in *T. S. Eliot: a Selected Critique,* ed. Leonard Unger. New York: Rinehart, 1948. pp. 374-394.

DATE DUE			
MAY 1 7 1991			
APR 0 0 1993			
APR 0 0 1993			